Getting Started

If you are discouraged because you don't think that you'll ever be able to afford your own home . . . if you're numb to the workaday humdrum . . . if you're unable to save, I've got just the elixir for you. Begin taking control of your financial future today. With as little as one weekend a month you can get started and achieve financial freedom in three or four years. I did . . . and I think you can, too!

Sophisticated real estate investors have made millions using the no down payment formulas. It's your turn to "cash in" on the coming real estate boom of the '80s. Get excited and make the decision that today will be the first day on your path to financial freedom.

Take control, turn the page, and set the stage for the circumstances of your real estate empire.

NO
DOWN PAYMENT
FORMULAS

by
Ed Beckley

BANTAM BOOKS
NEW YORK · TORONTO · LONDON · SYDNEY · AUCKLAND

*This edition contains the complete text
of the original hardcover edition.*
NOT ONE WORD HAS BEEN OMITTED.

NO DOWN PAYMENT FORMULAS

*A Bantam Book / published by arrangement with
the author*

PRINTING HISTORY
Midwest Financial Publications edition 1986

*Bantam edition / November 1987
3 printings through August 1989*

Illustrations by Don Day Studio

In this book I have used the male gender in illustrating most of the examples. I have not done this due to any inherent chauvinism, but only in an effort to keep things simple. Thanks for your tolerance.

ISBN 0-553-26986-0

Published simultaneously in the United States and Canada

---

*Bantam Books are published by Bantam Books, a division of Bantam
Doubleday Dell Publishing Group, Inc. Its trademark, consisting of the
words "Bantam Books" and the portrayal of a rooster, is Registered in U.S.
Patent and Trademark Office and in other countries. Marca Registrada.
Bantam Books, 666 Fifth Avenue, New York, New York 10103.*

PRINTED IN THE UNITED STATES OF AMERICA

O   12 11 10 9 8 7 6 5

Table of Contents

NO
DOWN PAYMENT
FORMULAS

CHAPTER 1
Starting from Scratch

In 1975, I had a job teaching at a small high school in northern California. My wife and I had a dream. It was a small dream: We wanted to own our own home. We had only one minor problem . . . or we *thought* it was a problem. We couldn't save enough money from my salary for the required down payment.

From time to time we would visit realtors, inquiring about the local housing market. It was definitely headed up. It seemed prices, down payments, and monthly payments were heading out of our reach. Local realtors would give us this line: "You need at least $4,000 for a down payment or you might as well forget about looking." We were really discouraged.

We made a sincere effort to save . . . but to save $4,000 would have taken us years on my salary. If you've attempted to save money in the current economic conditions, then you know what I mean. It's darned hard to save money these days! Besides, we figured that by the time we had accumulated that "magic" $4,000 down payment, prices would have skyrocketed further . . . raising the required down payment again.

The problem with saving was that each time we accumulated $1,000 in our savings account, an unexpected expense would pop up. You know the kind I mean . . . hospital bills for having babies, new tires for the car, braces for the kids, replacing those worn socks.

We were ready to give in to what I called the *Renter's Financial Bondage.* The renter finds it very difficult to accumulate any personal wealth during his lifetime. When Mr. Renter makes that monthly rent payment, the money is gone. When Mr. Homeowner makes his mortgage payment, he is beginning to create a firm foundation of personal wealth.

MENTAL PROSPERITY: THE KEY TO SUCCESS

My personal discouragement led me to begin reading various "How To Get Rich" books. I began to think that if we *couldn't* save for that down payment, perhaps some of the so-called "experts" had some special real estate secret that we might be able to use.

In Napoleon Hill's book, *Think and Grow Rich,* I found that first bit of wisdom . . . those secrets for which I had been searching. I read "Whatever the mind of man can conceive and believe, it can achieve." That was a shot in the arm!

When I read that statement, an important realization came to me. We hadn't bought our first home because we never really believed it was possible. It was just a dream!

A dream without the belief that it will really come true will remain only a dream. To truly realize our dreams in life, we must have sincere belief. If we look within and overcome fear and doubt, positive thinking results. Positive thinking cultures our ability to sincerely believe and achieve!

I knew then that I had to change my thoughts. I knew that I had to sincerely believe that we could own our own home. Thoughts are habits that can be changed or altered. Most people don't succeed at whatever they do simply because of the limitations they put on their thinking. They go through life telling themselves, "I guess I can't do it," rather than, "How can I do it?"

I began to read real estate books. William Nickerson's *How I Turned $1000 Into $1,000,000 In My Spare Time* was my first book. This book is probably responsible for more real estate millionaires than any other I know. This great book gave me so much valuable information that the boundaries to my thinking were being "blown apart" with each chapter. I had made another decision. I wasn't just going to buy a house, *I was going to be rich* . . . and real estate was going to get me there. I was going to create a real estate empire.

I began devouring every "tidbit" of real estate information that I could get my hands on. I read more books . . . listened to tapes . . . talked with and quizzed real estate people until they were ready to throw me out of their offices. I subscribed to magazines and newsletters.

During this period of study, I kept coming up with the same astonishing conclusion. *You don't need money to buy real estate, you need knowledge.*

SUBSTITUTING IDEAS FOR CASH

I now had all the tools I needed to go out and begin to build my real estate empire. It was time to do it!

My shortage of cash was still there. I knew that my first challenge would be to *substitute ideas for cash*. I used a very basic no down payment formula, which you'll read about in the chapter called "Pulling Money Out of a Hat," to make the first offer. The offer was accepted. We were the proud owners of a nice two-bedroom house with a spacious view. Our dream had become a reality. We had truly created that house in our life from ideas.

Money is not always necessary . . . ideas are the "backbone" of all successful wealth-building programs. I found this theme time and time again while reading stories of how great men made their fortunes.

Let's Get Another One

The first house was so easy to buy, we decided to use our ideas to acquire more property. Why? We looked at some of the financial benefits real estate could bring us.

1. Appreciating value

2. Equity buildup

3. Tax shelter

4. Income

Yes, we were excited and eager to begin building our real estate empire. We had made a definite decision that real estate investment was the way to get rich. After all, if ideas were all we needed to buy property, our plan was simple: When we found the right property, we had only to come up with the necessary ideas. *Money wasn't our main concern.*

Onward to a Million

In the next three years we acquired over two million dollars in real estate. Much of this was purchased using the no down payment formulas you'll be reading about in this book.

During these three years, I adopted a fundamental buying philosophy. It's called the *Conservation of Cash Philosophy*. Never use your own cash to buy property if at all possible. Your cash will vanish quickly enough in today's economic conditions. This philosophy is the fundamental basis of the book.

By using the Conservation of Cash Philosophy, our wealth pyramided to a point where I decided to quit my schoolteaching job. It was a great day! That day I was able to declare financial freedom. My decisions in life began to change. Would I continue to make more money . . . create more wealth! Would I travel, go off to meditate for a while, or would I just stay home and loaf? I was no longer a slave to a job. I had a choice!

Do You Want that Choice?

I wrote this book so you might have a greater degree of choice in your life. When I speak of choice, I mean two things: What you do with your time, and the ability to have the things you want in life without them being a financial burden—such as nice cars, trips to Hawaii, boats, or just solitude. Having financial freedom expands the range of your choice. How much control do you exercise over your life?

The only chance most people get to exercise much choice over what they do with their time is when they retire. The only trouble is that ninety-five percent of the people in our country retire almost broke. They're unfortunately on an inadequate Social Security dole. Their time is free, but they don't have the money to use that time the way they had dreamed they would. They work hard all of their lives enslaved in that nine-to-five drudgery. The dream of retirement is the only thing that keeps them going. When they finally retire, they don't have the money to enjoy that free time. Is that what you want? Do you intend to remain in the same rut as most people, who are too busy earning a living to ever make any money?

You can work hard all your life and wind up broke. Learn to work smart! The greatest myth in our country goes like this: Go to school so you can get a good job which will give you financial security. If that were true, all the old people in this country would be very wealthy. Yet, according to the Social Security Board of the United States government, ninety-eight out of one hundred folks at age 65 are either broke, dependent upon government or family handouts, or still have to work. Have you bought that American myth for you and your family?

GET STARTED TODAY

In *No Down Payment Formulas* you're going to learn how to buy real estate without using your own money. You'll use the dynamic secret of O.P.M.—other people's money. You'll see the practical application of the Conservation of Cash Philosophy—cash is a rare commodity, always preserve it—and you're going to discover how to substitute the over one hundred No Down Payment ideas in this book for cash.

Most of all, I want you to have this information so that you can begin to exercise more choice over your life. If you are discouraged because you don't think that you'll ever be able to afford your own home . . . if you're numb to the workaday humdrum . . . if you're unable to save . . . if you're tired of life, I've got just the elixir for you. Begin taking control of your financial future today. With as little as one weekend a month you can get started and achieve financial freedom in three or four years. I did . . . and I think you can, too!

Sophisticated real estate investors have made millions using the no down payment formulas. It's your turn to "cash in" on the current real estate boom. For these formulas to work, you're going to have to put forth a little creative effort. Neil Gustafson, a famous real estate investor, once said: "Any damn fool can buy property with money, it takes creativity to buy without money."

Get excited and make the decision that today will be the first day on your path to financial freedom.

Disraeli said: "Man is not the creature of circumstances, circumstances are the creatures of men." Take control, turn the page, and set the stage for the circumstances of your real estate empire.

POINTS TO REMEMBER

- Change your thoughts today. Be the architect of your own future.

- Gain knowledge. Knowledge is power.

- You don't need money to buy real estate, you need knowledge.

- Substitute ideas for cash.

- Adopt the Conservation of Cash Philosophy.

- Exercise more choice over your life today.

- You create your own circumstances. Decide today that your future will be in real estate . . . and begin.

CHAPTER 2
Is Real Estate Still the Ideal Investment?

Since our forefathers signed the Declaration of Independence in 1776, real estate has been the most consistently performing investment. Of course, you need to choose the right real estate investments . . . but I'll show you how to spot these later. During our over two hundred years' experience with real estate as a medium of investment in the United States, there have been slow phases. One thing we do know for certain, real estate has *always*

bounded back. It has been the long-time investment winner. Fundamentally, it is the basis of all wealth!

The factors contributing to the inexorable march of real estate prices never rest. I've been asked, "What if there is zero appreciation in real estate prices?" Given the historical evidence that housing prices have gone up in eighty-two out of the last eighty-six years, I rate a complete flattening of housing prices as highly unlikely. However, if prices did stabilize for a period of years, simply use the techniques in this book to purchase properties under market value. The real estate market is an open arena for negotiating transactions. You can't pick up a newspaper and find out the current price of your home. As a result, bargains exist for those who have market knowledge.

The time to buy any investment is when the public mood appears not to favor it. The media has a funny way of picturing the world the way it isn't . . . that's why I used the word "appears." *The time to buy is now.*

Now, I'd like to tell you why I think that real estate is still the most dynamic investment vehicle for getting rich. Why it will be in the future . . . and why now is the great golden opportunity to buy.

WHY REAL ESTATE IS STILL
THE NUMBER ONE INVESTMENT

Inflation is with us to stay. Housing has traditionally been, and will continue to be, a good hedge against inflation. In fact, in most areas well-located houses have risen in price faster than inflation. I bought a little two-bedroom house in 1975 for $19,000. Today, its estimated market value is $65,000. Its value more than tripled in a nine-year period. We paid full market value and never really did any major improvements to it. We made $46,000 by simply buying and letting inflation do its thing.

Why is housing so sensitive to general price rises in our economy? Basically, Uncle Sam has elected to print lots of money to help all those people who can't help themselves. (They should read this book.) He's a kindly uncle with good intentions. The problem is that he is giving more money away than he has. Everybody has Uncle Sam's money. In fact, so many people have his money that when they buy something with it they bid against each other. They pay more and more dollars just to get their wealth out of dollars into commodities such as housing, food, cars, TV sets, etc. There are more dollars around than commodities, so prices (dollars paid) for commodities rise . . . too much money chasing too few goods.

If you didn't understand that explanation, don't worry about it, it won't hurt you in your pursuit of financial freedom. It might only help you begin to understand why you're getting rich.

In our economy today, we have spent all this money trying to acquire the limited necessary resources needed to build a house. These items include labor (when's the last time wages fell remarkably?), lumber, concrete, etc. As materials and labor costs continue to rise, you can depend on the cost of new housing to rise. This pushes up the prices of older, existing housing.

Local government red tape tends to delay construction dates and saddle the builder with costly building requirements. Delays cost more money because as time goes on, materials and labor costs also rise . . . this adds increasing upward pressure to housing prices.

Uncle Sam expects inflation. He indexes government pensions, Social Security payments, and some salaries to the Consumer Price Index. Bankers expect it; that's why these big money merchants are adopting variable rate mortgages. The fixed-rate, long-term mortgages just won't make money for them in inflationary times. Some labor unions have a cost of living escalator worked into their contracts year in and year out, and big business budgets inflation as an annual cost of doing busines. The vicious cycle goes on!

For the last 20 years our leaders in Washington have been trying to keep inflation under control. I hope they will achieve this important goal, but frankly, I am not betting on it. For the sake of this example, however, assume that they could succeed in maintaining a very modest 4% inflation rate. That means that if you bought a

house today for $80,000 and its price kept pace with infla-
tion, its price in six years would be over $100,000. (4% ×
$80,000 = $3,200. So the price at the end of one year with
4% appreciation would be $83,200. In the second year the
house's value would go up $3,328 (4% × $83,200) to
$86,528. If you keep going that way, by the end of the
sixth year the house would be worth just over $101,000.)

Will Rogers' famous quote, "Invest in inflation, it's the
only thing going up," rings as crystal clear today as it did
when it was first said. Don't become the victim of inflation; use its momentum to change your financial future in
the '80s. Buy today!

Continuing Demand for Housing

Loaded with the high expectations of the homeownership
dream, forty-two million would-be homebuyers are going
to be demanding their own homes in the next ten years.
They might accept less, such as a smaller home, but they
do want decent shelter.

Will Rogers also said, "Invest in land, they ain't making
any more." Houses have to sit on land. Land is a limited
commodity. As more and more people need shelter in
desirable areas of the country, what do you suppose will
happen to the demand for that scarce commodity, good
land? When you've got heavy demand, prices go up.

Tax law changes are also affecting the demand and
supply situation for rental housing. The tax law changes
provide a disincentive for the construction of new rental
properties. But we all know that the population is continuing to increase and that means that demand for housing
must also continue to increase. This increasing demand,
coupled with insufficient supply of housing, will cause
higher rents. The good news is that, if you are a landlord,
the higher rents will give you more dollars in your pocket
each month . . . higher cash flow. Cash flow is what
creates independence!

People demand good housing whether they rent or
buy. Shelter at an affordable price is a fundamental hu-
man need—like food and clothing. Look at your local

newspaper ads under the column titled "Houses For Rent." Compare those columns with newspapers from two or three years ago. You'll notice that available rentals are probably getting "slim." This is just another indicator of the chronic housing shortage that is developing. The demand is there! Let's look at some of the reasons why I think a new wave of financial tools will continue to bring affordable mortgage money into the market.

NEW WAVE OF FINANCIAL TECHNIQUES

It's no secret that in the last few years banks and savings and loans have been in trouble. They've been caught in the old game of borrowing for the short term and lending long term. In tight-money times, these lending institutions have to pay more (higher interest rates) to attract funds through various savings plans than they receive in yield from their old long-term fixed-rate loans. You know the kind that I mean . . . eight percent, thirty years to pay. The problem is that institutions, at various times, have had to pay ten or twelve percent interest to keep attracting would-be savers. The days of strolling into your friendly savings and loan and getting a long-term low-interest loan to buy a house disappeared a number of years ago. (But the opportunity for low-interest loans was and is still there when dealing with owners . . . I'll show you how in a later chapter.) It just didn't pay the money merchants to do that anymore. However, times change, and the money merchants are once again offering long-term fixed-rate mortages.

Don't fret, though. Money (wealth) does not disappear . . . it just flows toward the area of greater attractiveness. Savings institutions in this country are designing programs so that an abundance of mortgage money once again will flow into their coffers. Uncle Sam even wants to help. His attitude is to encourage more savings through tax incentives and eliminate assumable loans. These are just a couple of the strategies being implemented. His whole idea is to once again create enough mortgage money at agreeable terms. A society of homeowners is a happy, stable populace, particularly when you figure that most of the wealth people have accumulated in a lifetime is tied up in their homes. I even read recently that the state of Alaska was subsidizing a bond issue so they could offer six percent mortgage money for first-time homebuyers.

With this favorable Washington attitude, and the necessities of the current economic climate, new ideas had to arise. The lending institutions of this country used a fundamental wealth-building and -conserving premise.

Money Flows Toward Ideas

Mr. Banker knew that if he once again was going to be the premier money merchant in town, he'd have to come up with some pretty handy ideas . . . and that he did. A whole shopping basket full, guaranteed to supply you with all the mortgage money you'll need at *initial* "affordable" prices.

These new mortgage programs are called Shared Appreciation Mortgages, Variable Rate Mortgages, Renegotiated Rate Mortgages, Graduated Payment Plans, and other names. These programs have to work, or the money merchants are out of business.

Another financial tool arising from the private sector is the equity-sharing programs. Many owners in these tight-money times are more receptive to carrying the financing on their property. I'll go into more detail on these programs in a later chapter.

Innovations from the money merchants will still provide money at an acceptable price to fuel the housing boom of the '80s. We've got inflation to help us and people need and want housing. The money merchants are standing by to fuel this housing boom . . . or they're out of business.

TAX INCENTIVES

Real estate investment in improved property still provides one of the most outstanding tax shelters available today. One of the keys to the real estate tax shelter is depreciation. Basically, the I.R.S. lets you deduct a portion of the improvements on the land, such as a house, apartment building, etc. You can take this expense each year over the "useful life" of that improvement. You can't depreciate land . . . only improvements to the land. Let's say that you bought a nice rental house for $75,000. Your accountant determines that $25,000 will be allocated for the land and $50,000 will be the value of the improvements. Using a simple straight-line method of depreciation, if you use an estimated twenty-seven-and-a-half-year life for the house, you divide your $50,000 by the twenty-seven-and-a-half-year life. This gives you a $1,818 deduction per year that the I.R.S. calls a reserve for "depreciation." You can deduct that $1,818 each year on your tax return for the estimated life of the house. That could mean hundreds of dollars each year in your pocket through tax savings, depending on your tax situation. (You can only enjoy full deduction of depreciation if your income is below a certain level. Otherwise, you can carry excess deductions backward and/or forward to reap your full benefits.)

Does Real Estate Really Depreciate in Value?

In actuality, you know that your rental house isn't depreciating in value . . . or you should know that, by now. It's appreciating at the inflation rate. Depreciation is a "phantom expense." This phantom expense is such a great tax shelter. The I.R.S. might even let you carry some of your excess depreciation losses back three years. You could even get a refund from past taxes that you paid. What a way to get started on pyramiding your real estate empire!

The tax incentives alone will attract millions of our overtaxed workers to real estate investment as a means of putting hundreds and even thousands of extra dollars into their pockets each year.

As you watch your earnings and dollars getting chewed up by taxes, think about the money that you could save by buying one little rental house today. That phantom expense, depreciation, is there waiting for you to tap its wealth.

LEVERAGE: THE TOOL TO MAKE MILLIONS

Archimedes said, "Give me a lever long enough and a prop strong enough, and I can single-handedly move the world."

Leverage is one of the dynamic keys that makes real estate one of the best ways a "small" guy can still make a million dollars. Basically, leverage is a method used to control a lot of property with little or no money. You can control a nice piece of real estate without using any of your own cash. This is called infinite leverage. You're going to learn to control appreciating real estate with the ideas in this book. Understanding how to effectively use infinite leverage is the central theme of this book.

Mark C. Understood the Power of Using Infinite Leverage

In a two-year period, Mark was able to buy almost three million dollars worth of good developable land, all without using any of his own money. How did he do this, you ask? He understood the use of syndicated options. I'm going to show you how to duplicate Mark's success in the chapter on options. In a little over two years Mark's net worth soared to one and a half million dollars. Not bad for a guy starting with no money and a simple idea. He did it . . . you can do it. Get determined today. You see, Mark understood the dynamic wealth-building ability of leverage. But he also understood another vital principle in our no down payment philosophy: O.P.M., Other People's Money. Always utilize somebody else's money when you are buying a real estate investment. You provide the ability to find and structure the project, somebody else provides the cash. It's a win-win deal. Or, if you don't have the time, provide the cash and become a passive investor.

The investment experts don't mind going into what I call *creative debt*, if they smell a profit. Creative debt is a further refinement of O.P.M. You borrow money and you pay the going interest rate for that money. You take that money and, if you're wise, find a good real estate investment that will yield you in excess of the going interest rate.

Creative debt refines the O.P.M. philosophy by using only your knowledge to acquire property. You create the ideas, and the cash necessary to close the transaction will come. It will come when you provide the proper incentives to attract the partners and lenders necessary to compete the no down payment deal.

If you're making money on the borrowed funds, the interest rate is irrelevant. But watch out! Leverage is a double-edged sword. You can lose any investment or equity you have if you can't service the mortgage payments or other debts you signed in order to purchase the property. Use the prudent man rule: Before you leap into deep debt to acquire any property with leverage, be thorough with all your homework.

However, it is better to have tried. In California most purchase money loans that you sign to buy property are non-recourse, so that the lender almost never could go after your personal assets if something went sour. The only recourse most lenders have with purchase money mortgages is to take the property with which it is secured. In the conservation of capital philosophy we never have any cash of our own at risk. The most you can lose is your time. Remember that not to have tried is the real ultimate risk.

Let's look at the following table so that you can really get the full impact of using leverage in real estate. Let's say that by using the no down payment formulas you're going to learn in this book, you acquire $1,000,000 in real estate in the next year. Does that sound difficult? That's only ten medium-priced homes in the Los Angeles area . . . or fifteen houses in Sacramento. You'll have to work, but you can do it. Do you know how long it will take that million dollars in gross real estate assets to grow to one million in equity, for you to be a true millionaire? All you've got to do is hold on and let inflation do its thing.

Chart 1

Gross Assets	Inflation Rate					
	5%	**8%**	**10%**	**12%**	**14%**	**18%**
$1,000,000	14.5 yrs.	8.5 yrs.	7 yrs.	6 yrs.	5 yrs.	4 yrs.
500,000	22.6 yrs.	13.7 yrs.	11 yrs.	9 yrs.	8 yrs.	6 yrs.

The top line of this chart represents the inflation rate and the second and third lines correspond to the gross real estate assets you might purchase. For example, if today you acquired $1,000,000 in real estate with no down payment and assumed a ten percent inflation factor, it would take approximately seven years for you to gross equity of $1,000,000. You could become a millionaire in seven years.

Isn't that amazing? Where else can you find an investment that has shown such long-term consistency in appreciation, the bountiful tax advantages, and the ability to leverage yourself to millionaire status without working hard for forty years? Real estate investment allows you to work less and accomplish more. Perfection of economy. By the way, collect those books and articles pronouncing doom in real estate investment. These can be an excellent negotiating tool when you're attempting to get a favorable price and terms on a hot real estate investment. Throw books like Cardiff and English's *The Coming Real Estate Crash* on his office table and watch the seller's eyes bug out.

When you become a millionaire, you'll have achieved financial freedom. You can do as you wish, go where you want, and begin to pursue some of the higher goals in the universe . . . infinite wealth. The time to invest in real estate is today.

POINTS TO REMEMBER

- Real estate has been in a consolidating stage in the early 1980s.

- Buy now and reap the reward of the boom of the next five years.

- Inflation will ensure constantly rising prices.

- Demand for housing is outstripping the existing supply.

- People need shelter; this is fundamental.

- They're not making any more land.

- Tax shelter aspects in real estate make it a winner.

- A new wave of financial techniques provide affordable mortgage money.

- The power of leverage can make you a fortune.

- Use other people's money . . . you provide ability (ideas).

- Buy real estate today . . . be a millionaire empire builder tomorrow.

CHAPTER 3
Real Estate Empire Building Rules

To be a real estate empire builder, you've got to learn the rules of the game. An empire builder plans his moves, creates his own breaks, and overcomes all resistance with his attitude. Let's find out about the empire builder's sure-fire rules for success.

SET SPECIFIC GOALS

A couple of weeks ago my family and I decided to take a drive in the country. We had a vague idea of where we were going, but weren't real certain. After all, it was meant to be a fun family outing. We didn't take a map, and we didn't plan our route very well. We were having a good time exploring different roads without making much headway toward our destination. Pretty soon we found ourselves lost and real close to being out of gas.

Most people go through life like this! Don't they? A vague sense of where they are going . . . no map or plan to show them how to get to their destination . . . and what happens? Pretty soon they're lost in life with a sense of helplessness . . . and they've run out of gas. They don't seem to have the energy to change.

It doesn't have to be that way! Each time we take a breath, we have the potential to change. "But how?" you ask. By deciding exactly where you want to go in life and making a written plan of how and when you will arrive there.

Goals in life must be written! They must be specific and you must be committed to them to ensure success. The late billionaire J. Paul Getty said, "If you don't write down goals, it's just an excuse for not trying."

The first step toward building a real estate empire is finding out where you are right now, financially. You can't set realistic financial goals unless you know where you are right now. The best format I've seen for taking the pulse of your financial health is the bankers' financial statement. There is a copy of one of these on the next page. You can use this one, or go to your banker and ask for a financial statement. He'll be glad to give you one. In fact, you might sense a bit of excitement coming from him, as he thinks you might be applying for one of his high-interest-loan specials. Poor bankers, they're lonely nowadays. He'll be glad to see you.

When you get the form, fill it out immediately. No, not tomorrow. Today! If you're going to accumulate a real estate empire you've got to start now. After properly evaluating your present financial state, you're in a better position to decide on future financial goals.

Be specific with your goals. Decide on what you will do with your future wealth. Will you buy a red Ferrari? A

Lear jet? A mansion? Or do you just want a nice cabin in the mountains, where you can go and meditate without having to worry about money? Obviously, if you would rather have the latter, your financial goals might mean only accumulating a net worth of $100,000. With $100,000 invested, earning ten percent, you could reasonably expect a monthly income of over $800 per month. That might spell financial freedom for some. For others, a million dollars a year wouldn't be enough. It might be five million. I met a guy recently who had a goal to make thirty million by the time he was thirty. He is twenty-three and has already made his first million. He has made it in real estate, starting from scratch. That's thinking big!

Make Your Goals Positive and Specific

Such as: I will buy a three-bedroom, two-bath house, in a good neighborhood, by September 1, 19__. I will have a $1,000,000 net worth in real estate by July 1, 19__.

You'll notice two types of goals in the above statement. The first one mentioned is the *how* portion of the plan; the first goal illustrates the specific investment vehicle you'll use to build the $1,000,000 net worth. The second type will deal with the amount of that financial goal.

Set goals in short-term time blocks. Psychologists tell us that these shorter-time-period goals are most successfully accomplished.

I like to set weekly goals. These then fit in with monthly, quarterly, yearly, and final goals.

Commitment

After writing your goals, emotionally charge them by a special commitment to their attainment. You might try writing a commitment of this type: I hereby swear that I shall accomplish the goals by the date given. Then sign your name—you're committed! You can see the importance of being very clear about what you want and the price you are willing to pay to get it. All success in life demands a price. That price might involve a time commit-

Personal Financial Statement

Date _____

Instructions

You may apply for credit in your name alone, regardless of marital status. Check your marital status below only if (a) you live in a community property state, such as California, or (b) this is a joint application. You must answer the questions about your spouse only if you're married and (a) you live in a community property state, or (b) this is a joint application with your spouse.

☐ Married   ☐ Unmarried   ☐ Separated

If you're married and live in a community property state, _____ (the "Bank") will assume that all assets, income, and debts are community property, unless you indicate otherwise in the "Comments Section" on the reverse.

Joint or Individual/Separate Credit (check below):

☐ You are applying for individual credit

☐ You are applying for joint credit

☐ The joint applicant is a person who is not your spouse (complete two forms). Name _____

☐ The joint applicant is your spouse (complete one form). Name _____

NAME _____ AGE _____

SOCIAL SEC. NO. _____ HOME PHONE _____

STREET ADDRESS _____

CITY _____ STATE _____ ZIP _____

RECEIVED AT _____ BRANCH

EMPLOYED BY _____ YEARS _____

EMPLOYER'S ADDRESS _____ STREET ____ CITY ____ STATE ____ ZIP

BUSINESS PHONE _____ POSITION _____

IF EMPLOYED LESS THAN 1 YEAR, PREVIOUS EMPLOYER _____

TO: _____ To get and maintain credit with Bank, you furnish the following (and attached, if applicable) full and correct statement of your financial condition. It is the most recent, and Bank may assume it to be a continuing statement of your financial condition as of the date indicated. You will notify Bank immediately, in writing, if your financial condition changes in any important way. You also agree that all of your obligations to Bank, or held by Bank will immediately become due and payable, without demand or notice, if: 1) You or any endorser or guarantor of your obligations experience business failure, insolvency or bankruptcy, or any of you die; 2) an attachment or involuntary lien of any kind is issued against your assets or the assets of any endorser or guarantor of your obligations; 3) any information given on your financial statement or credit application proves to be untrue; 4) any important change occurs in your financial condition; 5) you fail to notify Bank of such change; or 6) your business, or any interest in it, is sold.

ASSETS	AMOUNT (Omit cents)	LIABILITIES	AMOUNT (Omit cents)
Cash		Notes Payable	
Cash in Other (give name)		Notes Payable to Other (give name)	
Accounts Receivable (Schedule C on reverse)		Accounts Payable to (give name)	
Stocks and Bonds (Schedule B on reverse)		1.	
Notes Receivable (Schedule C on reverse)		2.	
Cash Surrender Value Life Insurance		3.	
Autos (Year - Make)		4.	
Autos (Year - Make)		Taxes Payable	
Real Estate (Schedule A on reverse)		Real Estate Indebtedness (Schedule A on reverse)	
Household Goods		Other Liabilities (describe)	
Other Assets (describe)		1.	
1.		2.	
2.		3.	
3.		4.	
4.		5.	
5.		TOTAL LIABILITIES $	
		NET WORTH (Total assets minus total liabilities) $	
TOTAL ASSETS $		TOTAL LIABILITIES & NET WORTH $	

ANNUAL INCOME		ANNUAL EXPENDITURES	
Salary (Gross) - Applicant		Real Estate payment(s)	
Salary (Gross) - Spouse		Rent/Lease payment(s)	
Securities Income		Income Taxes	
Rental Income		Insurance Premiums (all types)	
Other (describe) I understand that I need not reveal income from alimony, child support or separate maintenance unless I want the bank to consider it when evaluating this statement.)		Property Taxes	
1.		Alimony, Child Support or Separate Maintenance	
2.		Other (describe - include installment payments other than real estate)	
3.		1.	
4.		2.	
		3.	
TOTAL INCOME $		TOTAL EXPENDITURES $	

LESS - TOTAL EXPENDITURES $ _____

NET CASH INCOME (Exclusive of ordinary living expenses) $ _____

CONTINGENT LIABILITIES (Debts on which you or your spouse is endorser, guarantor, or endorser and obligations which either of you will have to pay if the person primarily liable does not pay.)

1. _____
2. _____
3. _____

Is any of this income likely to be reduced or interrupted within the next year?

☐ Yes ☐ No   If yes, how long will the interruption last? _____

TOTAL $ _____

YOUR SIGNATURE

By signing below, you certify that the statements above and on any attachment(s) are true and complete as of the date given below. You authorize the Bank to verify or check any of the information given, check your credit references, verify employment and obtain credit reports (including your spouse, if you are married and live in a community property state). You also authorize the Bank to provide credit information about you and your accounts to others.

Date: _____ X _____ APPLICANT

Date: _____ X _____ APPLICANT

ment of a period of two or three years in your life. If you sincerely want financial freedom, be willing to pay that price. Be committed to the attainment of your goals. Commitment is essential for success.

Read your goals daily; twice a day is even better. It's best to read them when your mind is quiet, such as after meditation, prayer, a long walk, before bed, or after rising in the morning. A quiet mind is very receptive and generally very positive. It'll allow your subconscious mind to begin to orient all your thoughts, abilities, and energies toward the attainment of your riches.

There is some degree of flexibility with the goal-setting plan. No excuses, just use your discretion. Don't abandon the goals because you failed to achieve some part of them. Gently bring your attention back in focus with your goals and begin moving forward again. However, in the event your goals are not achieved in the allotted time period, adjust them to fit a more reasonable schedule. Don't give up! Keep making progress!

Get involved with your goals. Picture the houses you'll own; see the Rolls Royce you are going to buy; think about and feel the enjoyment.

I have a friend who has a goal of owning a Rolls Royce. He has cut out a picture of a Rolls from an ad he saw in a magazine. He's placed it at eye level in front of his desk. He's definitely seeing his goal, and my bet is that he gets it. Act like you already own that house, believe that you will accomplish your goal, and you will.

It has been said that all success is structured in preparation. Prepare your plan today so that you can enjoy the fruits of your real estate empire tomorrow.

Knowledge is Power

Bacon said, "For knowledge, too, is itself a power." Knowledge in real estate will give you the power you need to create your future fortune.

After you have set your goals, you are ready to go out in that big bad real estate market and begin to build your real estate empire, aren't you? Not so fast! That is like going off to war with a cork gun! Highly amusing, but not too effective. You need know-how!

Most of this book is dedicated to giving you the knowledge you are going to need to make money in real estate. Right now let us look at some of the real estate terminology that will be used in this book. This terminology will also be handy if you want to make some deals somewhere along the line. On the next page you will see some terms and their definitions. Study them until you feel familiar with them.

These terms will give you a start. We will go through others as they come up in later chapters. Also, it would be a good idea for you to get hold of a real estate license examination book for your state. I don't recommend getting a real estate license, but I do recommend learning some of the rules and terms of the game before you play. The better you know the rules, the better you play the game.

This book will provide you with most of the knowledge you'll need to make your million. However, there are other books, courses, seminars (including my No Down Payment Seminar), newsletters (my *Beckley Report*. See the back of the book for more information.), and lectures. There is a whole wealth of real estate knowledge in the marketplace today.

Actionize Knowledge

Use the knowledge as you learn it. Knowledge unused is sterile. Begin calling on ads in the real estate section in your paper, talk to local realtors, find people who have made it big in real estate, corner them, and absorb their financial wisdom. Remember, they did it! Find out how! As Ralph Waldo Emerson said, "Our knowledge is amassed through the experience of innumerable minds." By being dynamically involved with the rules, terms, and formulas of real estate, you will make it "lively" in your own awareness. You'll begin to truly know it.

Develop an idea reservoir. As you talk with people about real estate investment, a dynamic interaction will begin to take place. New ideas will blossom. These great ideas, formulas, and solutions have a way of slipping from our conscious grasp. Write them down as they come up and put them in an idea reservoir folder.

Utilize all those with whom you come in contact to gain more knowledge. Knowledge is the link between where you are now and your future fortune.

ADOPTING THE CREATIVE ATTITUDE

The innovator, the inventor, the problem solver, the creator, the genius—these are all words describing a person with a creative attitude. A person with a creative attitude seizes the essence of a problem, sees an opportunity, and proceeds to doggedly find a solution.

Thomas Edison said, "Genius is one percent inspiration and ninety-nine percent perspiration." Your imagination times dynamic action will bring you financial success. Creativity is basically the ability to solve problems in new and useful ways. Be unique, be novel in your approaches to real estate problems. In fact, you should be seeking out problems. You will find a pile of cash tied to the solutions.

When I drive down a block, I look for the messiest, doggiest, most slovenly unattended house. Why? Because the owners have got a problem. I see myself as a problem solver, with an "I can do it" attitude.

A little while ago I found such a house. It was an old Victorian. It looked awful—a real eyesore to the neighborhood. I found out that this house was being sold out of probate to settle an estate. The house was structurally sound, but was badly in need of paint, some carpeting, and a general cleanup job. I was able to buy the house well below market value because of apparent maintenance problems.

I used a local youth group to help me inexpensively paint it, clean it up, and perform the necessary repairs. In six months, I was able to resell that Victorian for a $20,000 profit, all because I was willing to creatively solve a problem. One person's problem is another person's opportunity. More importantly, I was looking for a problem. In

Escrow Company	This generally refers to a third party such as an attorney or title company which handles the paperwork for a real estate transaction.
Deposit Receipt	This is the form used as the basic real estate contract in California.
Note	This is an I.O.U. It can be unsecured (meaning if I default you have to come after my personal assets) or secured (meaning if I default you get the security). In this case, the security would be real property.
Deed of Trust	In real estate, this is the basic security agreement. It says simply that if you default on your note, I get your real estate. We can be very creative with this document. This term will be used interchangeably with mortgages in this book. Also, we use T.D. or Trust Deed for short.
Earnest Money	This refers to money you put down when you make an offer. This can be one dollar, or a postdated check, or a promissory note. Generally, it is $100 to $500.
Trustor	The person who owes money on the note secured by the Trust Deed.
Trustee	Usually a third party, such as a Title Company, an attorney, etc.
Beneficiary	This refers to a person who owns the note secured by the Trust Deed.
Grant or Warranty Deed	This is the document that grants title to a property.
Title Insurance	Title companies issue an insurance policy basically insuring that the title to the property is good.

time you will be a problem solver, too. David D. Edward said, "Inspiration favors the prepared mind." I might further modify this statement by saying, "Real estate profits favor the prepared mind."

It's Easy to Be Creative

Creative people dwell on the positive! Instead of, "It can't be done," the creative person might say "How can it be done?" Be solution-oriented! Find out the facts and solve the problem. There is always a solution!

Creative people question! They attempt to get at the heart of the problem. The facts surrounding the problem almost always are the keys to the solution. Cultivate a probing mind. When a seller says, "I need all cash for my property!" ask, "Why?" His answers will generally suggest some noncash solution to his problems.

Creative people see things in a unique way! They have an ability to see the whole problem, yet pick out aspects of the problem that suggest novel solutions. They are willing to look at the dilemmas from different angles and estate problems with different words.

Creative people are committed to solutions! In this book you are going to learn how to make money by solving problems. Persist with your solutions! Most people don't. If you persist in attempting to find solutions to real estate investment problems, you will find answers nobody else thought of, and you will make lots of money and have lots of fun doing it.

Creative people integrate and combine seemingly unrelated facts to arrive at solutions! For example, I have a friend who wanted to purchase a nice little rental. The price was good. The terms weren't. The seller wanted high-monthly-payment carryback note as part of his equity. This high-monthly-payment note would have generated significant negative cash flows (paying out more than was being taken in from rental income). My friend simply could not afford this.

The deal was about to fall through when my friend remembered a little-mentioned fact about the seller's life. The seller was planning to retire in five years. A light went on in my friend's brain. He remembered the Single Payment Note Formula. This concept will be explained in more detail in a later chapter. But basically, it is a note without monthly payments and with the principal and accrued interest due at the end of some time period, in this case, five years. My friend showed the seller the benefits (tax plus forced savings for retirement) of this type of financing. The seller went for it, and the deal was made.

The deal was made because my friend had that lively creative attitude. He took two sets of unrelated facts and used them to make a deal; also, his determination to find a solution brought him another step closer to his real estate empire.

WAYS TO DEVELOP A CREATIVE ATTITUDE

1. Meditate. I practice Transcendental Meditation®. It keeps my mind clear and alert. Also, when meditating, a calmness settles over the mind. This calmness is fertile ground for creative ideas. Many of my most creative ideas and solutions have come after meditation. Try it!

2. Spend some quiet time alone each day to gain perspective on your goals, problems, and new directions. A quiet walk in the woods, in the park, or by the ocean might be just right for you. These places have great calming effects on the mind. A busy mind breeds confusion and fear. A calm mind breeds positiveness and results.

3. Alter your routines periodically. Take a different route home. Get up earlier than normal one day a week. The early morning is a good time to be creative. Try to look at the same old houses on your way home. Look at them in different ways: "I wonder if that property could be rezoned commercial." "If that guy painted and landscaped that house, he could get $10,000 more than he's asking." Question and probe in new ways and perspectives.

4. Exercise. Rousseau said, "A feeble body weakens the mind." If you want a lively creative mind, you need a lively body. Besides, if you don't stay in good physical shape, what good will your millions do you? Well, at least you could rest assured that you could afford the best cardiac specialist. Great consolation . . . keep fit!

5. Keep an idea reservoir. Ideas come and ideas go. Have you ever had a great idea, a solution to a problem, an invention, an idea for a book, a new angle to an old dilemma? If you are like me, those ideas soon leave if you don't write them down. You would be surprised how valuable a file labeled "Idea Reservoir" could be in your real estate investment program.

6. Find humor in everything. Find an excuse to laugh. Find a person who gets a boot out of life, and I will show you someone who dwells on the positive and the unique.

DYNAMIC ACTION: THE CORNERSTONE OF SUCCESS

Ralph Waldo Emerson said, "Ideas must work through the brains and arms of good and brave men or they are no better than dreams."

You can have the clearest, most detailed set of goals that ever existed. You can acquire all the real estate knowledge available today. You can exhibit the liveliest creative attitude in the universe, but if you don't get off your fanny and "do it," you will never achieve anything.

Creative knowledge times dynamic action will bring you the wealth you desire. You are your own active instrument for success. Goals and the creative application of knowledge are lifeless without your direct action.

You have got to get out and look at houses, not just a couple of houses, but lots of them—maybe one hundred before you get to know the market well enough to make money.

REAL ESTATE SUCCESS STEPS

1. Action—Go out and make offers! You will never acquire your real estate empire without making an offer. It is time to stop dreaming about that first investment; make a creatively designed offer, and expect it to be accepted. Our own negative attitudes when we present the offer might create rejection. Our thoughts are forms that can support us or be our enemy. Be a positive force in the real estate marketplace. Expect acceptance! Smile, it is great medicine for yourself and those with whom you share it. A smile can melt the resistance of the most adamant seller's demands. Positive action breeds success.

2. *Momentum.* When you translate your goals to reality, when you begin making money with your real estate investments, you have established momentum. Keep it up! It will be fun, but one warning: Don't let up! Begin applying your diligent effort even more. Most people, upon making some nice profits from their initial real estate investment, make a big, crucial error. They do not reinvest their profits in real estate. They spend it on consumer items such as boats, cars, vacations, etc. They have just traded their appreciating asset for a depreciating one. There will be time for that kind of expenditure later. For now, keep up the momentum—reinvest. Repeat your success!

3. *Overcome Fear.* Madame Curie said, "Nothing in life is to be feared. It is only to be understood." Do your knees tremble when you think about going out in that big bad real estate world? Don't fret! You are not alone. However, if you sincerely want to create your real estate empire, you've got to do it. The most difficult time any of us do anything is the first time. Do you remember the first time you tried to ride a bike? I was sure scared, until I learned to ride. We don't know what is out there. Once we have done it, and understand it, the fear fades. Maharishi Mahesh Yogi says, "Knowledge is a great purifier." It purifies us of our fear! Besides, the ultimate fear is *not having tried!* I assure you, any fear you ever had will quickly depart as you achieve even small degrees of success.

4. *Persistent Action.* Persistence shatters resistance. Persist doggedly toward the accomplishment of your goals.

Elbert Hubbard said, "Genius is only the power to make continuous effort."

You might even meet some temporary defeat along your path to riches. I know that I have. Each time that I have met with temporary failure, I think of a quote from Napoleon Hill's fine book, *Think and Grow Rich.* "Every adversity, every failure, and every headache, carries with it the seed of an equivalent or greater benefit." Then I persist! Persistence and determination have been the powerful tools of successful men for thousands of years. Napoleon would never have gotten out of France without persistence, and Lincoln would not have held our nation together without a tenacious commitment to a goal.

The easiest thing to do is give up our goals, our aspirations, our future riches. Our family and friends would understand. They might say, "Oh, that's okay, your goals were too big! Sit your fanny down and let's watch the boob tube." What are they really saying? "Stay here in numbed mediocrity with me."

Persist in the investment and re-investment of well selected income property. You will have your financial freedom! You will overcome all obstacles in your path with persistence.

You should by now have a good vision of the rules by which a real achiever plays. The achiever, the real estate empire builder, takes full responsibility for the creation of his riches. As an old English proverb says, "Every man is the architect of his own fortune." With the effective application of the rules in this chapter, I assure you that financial freedom will be attained. Design your future financial goals today . . . and then do it!

CHAPTER 4
Mr. Motivation Needs Some Help

WHO IS MR. MOTIVATION?

He is an owner who's been awakened in the middle of the night three nights in a row by angry tenants demanding that he unplug their sewer. He is an owner who's getting the squeeze from the local collection agency. He is the owner who just got a job transfer to Iran.

Mr. Motivation simply wants out of his property. He is willing to take almost any offer, if he sees it solving his problem . . . and he wants that solution (offer) today, without any delays.

His reasons for selling generally are not profit-oriented. They are emotional! They are usually irrational! Many times Mr. Motivation is anxious to sell because of a temporary set of circumstances. Because of those circumstances, he is very flexible. He might take an airline ticket, a car, boat, your personal note, or just a handshake for his property. He will take whatever relieves the anxiety in his life.

People Problems, Not Property Problems.

These motivated people have a problem. You, being the empire builder searching out problems, can help. In fact, it is your duty as an empire builder to help solve problems.

Not all sellers have this type of motivation. In our current market, I think that you'll find about twenty percent of the sellers really want out of their property. These are the people on whom you want to concentrate your efforts. Don't get discouraged if your local real estate agent tells you that you won't find Mr. Motivation around here. You've got to do some digging to find him.

Gary Was Motivated

Gary was a successful contractor who organized a limited partnership to buy a nine-unit apartment building. The building was in need of remodeling. Gary proceeded to do this with the partnership funds and his own effort. He had gotten what he thought was an excellent buy on the property, because of its state of disrepair. He had found Mr. Motivation.

After the repairs were made, Gary proceeded to try to rent the apartments. He quickly discovered why Mr. Motivation was willing to let these units go so cheaply. He couldn't keep them rented; he couldn't collect rents from some tenants; he had evictions and vandalism problems.

He had a classic management problem. Management problems are probably the number one reason high-motivation sellers exist. Gary became Mr. Motivation himself . . . particularly after his made-in-heaven partnership began to squabble, and one of them filed a lawsuit. Gary was fed up and just wanted out. He took some gemstones (sapphires, topaz) for his equity . . . and was happy about it.

He confided in me after the transaction was over what a damper that nine-unit building had put on his life. His creativity suffered, he was uptight in general, and this tended to injure his other projects. When his problem was solved, his anxiety was relieved. What about the buyer? The buyer is now in the process of solving the management problem and fixing the place up again. Why do I think that this buyer will solve the management problems, when at least two others couldn't? I don't know that he can. But I do know that the building is in a fair location and is structurally sound. I think that if the management problems can be solved, that nine-unit building will be a gold mine.

One solution I would use is to find a good management company to straighten out the tenants and rent the vacant apartments. They're professional. Use their expertise to build your empire. Once the management headaches are relieved, a budding Mr. Empire Builder will be well on his way to financial freedom.

THE PROBLEM-SOLVING ATTITUDE

As I said before, to build a real estate empire you need to develop a problem-solving attitude. You need to search for owners who have problems. More importantly, you have to pay the price to relieve the seller's anxiety. In this book, I am going to give you over one hundred formulas designed to solve unique problems in the real estate marketplace. However, these formulas will be useless unless you are able to spot situations into which they will fit;

your efforts to use combinations of these formulas will compound your ability to take advantage of opportunities as they arise.

Don't be like Gary, who took on a problem to solve, only to have it become a problem in his life. I have been guilty of this myself. Find out early why the owner is selling. If massive structural repair is needed, stay away from it. That's an expensive problem to solve. It probably isn't worth your time or investment. There are too many good deals out there! A management problem is a good solvable problem, if you get the proper help or if you have the required grit. Actually, I recommend that budding empire builders manage their own properties when they first get started. Front-line experience will be invaluable as you grow. Drummond said, "Property has its duties as well as its rights." You'll know that soon enough when you manage your own rental property.

Five-Step Dynamic Solution Method

I approach a seller with a problem in a five-step process.

1. I try to find out what the problem is. "Why are you selling?" I ask questions that attempt to zero in on the *real* reason for selling (I've developed a battery of questions to gain maximum knowledge about the problem. You'll see these in the next chapter). "Do you have a debt problem?" "Are you retiring soon?" This is the fact-gathering part.

2. Brainstorm all possible solutions to the problem. That is, write down every thought you have about relieving the seller's anxiety. Don't judge the merit of your solutions, just write. It's also good to do this when you are just formulating the definition of the problem.

3. I list what they told me was needed. If they say they need all cash—*find out what they're going to use that cash for.* Answers to this question can give you the means to eliminate or reduce cash from the transaction: "Mr. Motivation, what will you buy with your expected cash?" Usually you can get him what he wants using your credit, abilities, and barter expertise. Substitute ideas for cash.

4. I write down in the clearest, simplest language exactly the nature of the problem. The sellers are getting a divorce! The seller has a terminal case of being a deadbeat. Formulate a clear statement defining the problem.

5. Come up with at least six solutions to the seller's problem. Some solutions will be more practical than others. Rank them in order of desirability. For example, you may have met with a seller who has $4,000 in delinquent consumer debts. The collection agency is making life miserable for him. The squeeze is on! If you solve Mr. Motivation's debt problems, you've got the house at a below-market price with very favorable terms.

Let's look at six possible solutions:

- Call collection agency to assume his debt; try for lower payments; offer additional collateral as an incentive.

- Get a partner to pay off debts. You could probably negotiate a discount on the payoff. Give the partner a percentage ownership in the house.

- Go to your bank and borrow the money on a longer term with lower payments, and negotiate to pay off the collection agency at a discount.

- Give seller a personal note equal to whatever his monthly debt obligations are. With some intimidation on your part, you might be able to get the collection agency to lower repayment schedule.

- Give seller your car and pay off his debts; borrow against seller's house to pay off debts (at a discount, of course).

- Put his debts on your charge card.

Do you get the idea? The ideas for structuring a real estate transaction are infinite. People sell their property because they need something! Find out what it is that they

need, and give it to them. To be a probem solver is to be
an empire builder. Find a problem today and solve it!

SELLERS WITH A PROBLEM

*1. Divorce generally creates a desperate need to dispose
of mutually held property.* Try to design two separate
packages so that each individual's needs are considered.
Remember that in a divorce, each ex-spouse could deed
you their fifty percent interest in their jointly held property without the other's permission. Check on how title is
vested before you assume this type of deal.

*2. Partnership breakups develop a lot of emotionally
motivated sellers.* Partners have a way of getting mad at
one another whenever things don't go precisely as planned.
I know a guy who spends most of his time picking up the
pieces of partnerships that have gone awry.

*3. Management problems lead the list of why owners be-
come Mr. Motivations.* Some of the most common management problems in real estate center around the following:

- Vacancies

- Too much geographic distance to manage

- Deferred maintenance

- Tenant hassles

- Rent collection

*4. Job transfers might create motivation in even the
seasoned investor.* Try to manage or supervise management of an apartment house a thousand miles away. It's
difficult under the best of circumstances.

5. The seller might be in foreclosure. That means he could
lose his entire equity if a buyer isn't found quickly. The
best time to approach a seller who is in foreclosure is
sometime prior to it going on sale. If it goes to sale, you
might get the property at a good price, but the terms
would be stiff—all cash. This might be difficult if you

haven't developed a quick source of cash through your banker or a friend. If you meet with the sellers prior to the sale, you have got some motivated people with whom to work. They might accept extremely creative terms with some flexible carryback financing. Perhaps you could trade them a recreational lot that's highest and best use is holding the earth together, a personal note, or you name it. They are not in a position to drive a hard bargain. I've bought several foreclosures in this manner, usually at thirty percent under market . . . that's called buying at a profit.

6. The seller might have high negative cash flows on a property. Many of these people are running out of cash to feed their alligator. There are ways of taming that alligator's appetite. (See the chapter on handling negative cash flow.) But beware! Don't run around collecting a lot of negative cash flow properties in your beginning stages of empire building, unless you have a high cash flow or you feel that you can solve the high payment problem within a reasonable time frame.

7. Probates and estate sales offer a fertile ground for Mr. Motivations. Many times the heirs who inherit property do not have the slightest interest in keeping it. They want the money . . . a monthly income . . . a car or boat. What they don't want is hassle! I've made more money buying property out of probate than any other single method. Generally, it is best to strike a reasonable bargain with the executor or executrix through their attorney early in the probate proceedings. It will still have to be approved by the court, but a cooperative attorney can help minimize the bidding competition once it gets to court.

8. People who are ill, people who need to move to another geographic area, and people who need to pay medical bills have high motivation. This is a very sensitive area. You, being the dynamic problem solver, are needed to fill this type of person's needs, but at the same time, you can't shortchange yourself. People who are ill are extremely vulnerable. I know some people who could walk into a sick person's home and literally steal it. They've got a callus over their heart. An empire builder always tries to strike a comfortable bargain between his self-interest and his heart. Try to always arrange a win-win transaction. You'll sleep better at night, and in the long run you'll enjoy your wealth a lot more.

9. Debt problems are symptomatic of our "buy now, pay later" consumer society. Many people are now in hock up to their eyeballs. Being in heavy debt with no apparent means of repayment creates chronic psychological pressures. Find Mr. Motivation who had to hock his kid's bicycle seat last week to keep the electricity on, and you'll find a very flexible seller.

10. People who lose their jobs many times opt to sell their home as an answer to their food habit. They are addicted to eating! You might solve their food problem and monthly payments on the house for a short period of time. In exchange, you might ask for an option to buy part or all of their home. Did you know that there are places where you can use your credit card to buy food? Find them in your neighborhood. This type of food supplier might come in handy.

There are other situations that place owners of real estate in difficult positions. Difficult positions are exactly the place in which we want to find the seller. It gives us bargaining leverage. Other areas where you can find don't wanters or Mr. Motivations include:

- Retirees
- People with too many other time commitments
- Builders
- Wealthy owners
- People with I.R.S. liens against them
- People with judgments against them
- Panicky people whose property taxes are behind

- People who are facing bankruptcy

Now that you know who the twenty percent of all sellers are in this real estate marketplace, let's figure out where they can be found.

The Courthouse

The courthouse has a wealth of information about people who want or need to get out of a piece of real estate. Generally, in a prominent place, you will find all sorts of legal notices pinned on the wall in the courthouse. The law requires that when you get into trouble, it be advertised. You will find notices of trustee's sales (foreclosure notices), probate documents, bankruptcy filings, divorce papers, partitions of partnerships, tax sales, etc.

I have a friend who regularly goes by the courthouse and gathers all this information. He contacts the attorneys involved after he has seen the property. He gets plenty of super deals from this technique. He has no time to pursue other means of finding Mr. Motivation. His cash coffers are full from this single method.

If you want to do some digging in the courthouse, you can find lots of indirect information that will make you money.

- Check on condemnation proceedings

- Check on the tax records for delinquencies

- Check the tax records for out-of-state owners

- Check the planning and zoning departments for people who are in trouble on a subdivision project

- Check for old subdivisions that were divided but never sold

There is a gold mine in the courthouse. Use it to find those flexible sellers who will give you super deals.

The Attorney

A probate attorney can feed you enough deals to make you rich very quickly. During one six-month period in my investment career, I bought three properties out of probate at very favorable prices. I did some minor cosmetic work. After the work was done, I figured that I had just increased my net worth by almost $100,000. My total cash investment was $10,000 (borrowed on a personal note from my banker), and that included all the work for deferred maintenance. I did this part time! I figured that I made more money on that little project than I would have made teaching high school for five years. It got me to do some serious thinking about a change.

Attorneys also seem to be the central clearinghouse for most of the problems in our society today, such as divorce settlements, bankruptcy, foreclosures, etc. Go to an attorney and you will find all the problems you can handle. Check with several attorneys. Let them know what you are doing. Leave your name and have the attorney give you a call when Mr. Motivation drifts into his office.

The Newspaper

Sellers pay good money to advertise their problems, but you've got to know what to look for.

Rules for working with newspaper ads:

- Try to deal with the "for sale by owner" ads first. You will probably be able to negotiate a much more favorable deal without a real estate agent becoming involved. Besides, you don't have to come up with a cash commission.

- When you do deal with an agent, find a good one. If you call on an ad, and you get a dunce (you will know after just a few questions), ask to talk to a more experienced agent. If he or she insists on handling the deal, hang up. It won't be worth your time and aggravation.

You know a seller is asking for help when you read newspaper ads with headlines like these:

- *Fixer upper*

- *Retirement*

- *Behind in Payments*

- *Nothing Down*

- *Desperate*—If it's an ad placed by a real estate agent, it probably means that the owner is mildly motivated. If it's a F.S.B.O. (For Sale By Owner), he really means business.

- *Foreclosure*

- *10% Down*—If an agent advocates this, he really means just commission and closing costs.

- *Low Down*—This could mean anything, but it's generally worth calling.

- *Flexible Financing*

- *Owner Financing*—In today's market, this is what you want. This can be gold, and I'll show you how to mine it in the chapter entitled "Cooperative Financing."

- *Assumptions*—This combined with owner financing is what you want, provided you are assuming a low-interest, long-term loan.

- *Owner Moving*—Transferred.

Another way of using the newspaper to spot Mr. Motivation is to check the legal notices in your local newspaper. This will tell you who died, who's sick, who's going to die (this is high finance), who's getting divorced, who's filing bankruptcy, who's getting sued, etc.

You might want to place an ad such as this one in your local newspapers:

> I'll pay full price for your house in 24 hours as long as it's no down or low down with flexible terms. Call Ed 989-1693.

Problem	Where do you find them?
Divorce	Legal notice section of newspaper, courthouse, attorneys, classified ads, marriage counselor, real estate agents
Partnership	Courthouse (partitions), classified ads, real estate agents, attorneys, accountants, exchange meetings
Management	Real estate agents, spotting unattended property, accountants, property management firms, tax records (out-of-state owner), sheriff department (complaints), on apartment buildings, local apartment owners' association, courthouse (tax, utility liens, and foreclosure notices), classified ads, apartments and houses for rent column, rental agents, exchange meetings
Job Transfers	Rental agents, insurance companies, garbage collector, mailmen, tax records (out-of-state owners), finders at large companies in personnel departments, for rent columns, local schools, real estate agents
Foreclosures	Title companies, legal notices in newspaper, local legal newspaper, HUD, exchange meetings, lenders, FHA resales, collection agencies, courthouse, attorneys, ads in classifed, real estate agent
Negative Cash Flow	Real estate agent, accountants, attorney, collection agency, lenders, exchange meetings, classified ads
Probates and Estate Sales	Attorneys, legal section of newspaper, local title companies, insurance companies, legal newspapers, courthouse, obituaries, funeral homes
People Who Are Ill	Insurance companies, accountants, hospital finders, classified ads, real estate agents, hospital admissions, exchange meetings, lenders
Debt Problems	Real estate agent, attorney, accountants, collection agency, bankruptcy attorney, courthouse, classified ad, property tax records, credit bureau, lenders, I.R.S., courthouse (judgments, lawsuits)
Lost Job	Accountants, lenders, finders in large companies, newspaper articles (layoffs), classified ads, exchange meetings, real estate agent

You'll be surprised at the calls you get from this type of ad.

Real Estate Agents Can Be a Source of Great Deals

A good agent is hard to find. It means an agent who gets out and really works the market. He knows what a good buy is. You will need to interview a lot of agents before you find even one with whom you can work effectively.

Meet with the agent and give him specific requirements of what you are looking for: low or no down payment, flexible terms, but most importantly, the seller must be highly motivated. If the agent says those kind of sellers never come around, or "I've been in the business for twenty years and I have never seen a no down payment deal," pick yourself up and exit quickly. You've got the wrong agent.

Good agents will have what is known as pocket listings. Those are listings that never get into the Multiple Listing Book because they sell very quickly to one of the agent's favorite clients. You want to be one of those favorite clients.

Also, a good agent might be willing to write a lot of offers for you. I had an agent who wrote fifty offers for me in a two-day period. We went through the Multiple Listing Book and picked properties we felt met my specific requirements. This is called the shotgun approach to making offers. You spray the market with offers at your terms and price, with a contingency clause in each contract, "subject to inspection." You only go out and inspect the house after the offer is accepted. If you don't want the house, use the contingency clause to back out gracefully. Generally, I have found that you can get about one in ten offers accepted if you offer all cash and twenty percent below market. That success factor might increase in the current tight-money times.

Find a good agent, and he will be worth his weight in gold.

Tour for the "Dog"

The tour for the "dog" involves choosing a neighborhood in which you might consider buying. Drive through the neighborhood looking for the dog of the block. Find a house with overgrown weeds, in need of paint, boarded up, broken windows, and that is generally in a state of disrepair, and I'll show you a motivated owner. If it is vacant, you know that you've got a winner! Generally, you can negotiate a lower price for a fixer-upper of this sort than its price might warrant based on the cost to bring it to good repair.

For example, my friend Richard had refined the tour-for-the-dog technique to a science. He toured an area of town where he owned other rental houses. He spotted a house that looked like a real mess. He also saw a paper pinned to the door. It was a condemnation notice. Richard looked at the house and figured that for about $5,000 he could put the house back into good shape. Richard contacted the owner. The owner was disgusted with this situation and the unfavorable publicity it gave him. The owner was ashamed; Richard listened as the guy said, "I'll take anything for it."

Richard said, "Would you take $50?"

The guy said, "Sold."

Richard was able to fix up the house for under his $5,000 cost-of-improvement projection. One year later, Richard sold the house for $25,000. He put approximately $5,000, including his down payment, into his investment, and he pulled out $20,000—a nice profit for Richard. All because he found a dog and offered a ridiculous price . . . and the seller was not profit-oriented . . . and Richard was able to improve the value of the property in excess of his actual cash outlay.

It won't take very many of these deals to build Richard a solid real estate empire. He was a problem solver and was abundantly rewarded.

Find Mr. Motivation, Mr. Distressed Seller, Mr. Don't Wanter, Mr. Flexible. These are the people with whom you need to deal to quickly build your real estate fortune.

Mr. Motivation is very willing to transfer to you any possible monetary profit on his property if you will just relieve the anxiety in his life. Solve a people problem today, and you will be on your way to financial freedom.

CHAPTER 5

Qualifying the Seller:
The First Step of Negotiations

Your goal this week is to buy a single family house newer than ten years old. It must be in a good neighborhood, close to shopping, schools, and parks. It must have a long-term, fixed-rate assumable loan on it, and the owner must carry back some very favorable financing. You must see an opportunity to eliminate or sharply reduce your cash input into the project. In short, the seller must be motivated to sell!

You have created a picture of your first prospective real estate investment. Make sure that you carry around that mental picture with you until the purchase is made. You might even write down the description and read it several times a day.

The next step is to qualify the seller and his property. Find the seller first, and the property later. I have found that a difficult seller is a more significant barrier to a successful transaction than problems with a property— unless the house you are looking at happens to be located next to a sewage plant. I looked at such a house one time; the smell would curl the hair on your toes. The seller couldn't keep any tenant in there, it didn't matter how low the rent was. Pass on these!

USING THE TELEPHONE TO FARM

First, go through your local newspaper and circle the "for sale by owner" ads. By doing this you gain some control over the type of investment you want, i.e., single family house, and the area in which you prefer to buy, i.e., in which neighborhoods (in my local newspaper the various neighborhoods are divided into different classified columns). The following is a battery of questions designed to give you maximum information about the seller and his property. After asking the questions, if the seller of the property, the neighborhood, and the financing fit your picture, make an appointment to see the property the following night.

These questions have been systematically designed to find out whether or not the seller and his property qualify for the no down payment investment program and to give you a definite edge in the first round of negotiations. After these questions are answered, you will know if you want to proceed further. Make sure before you meet Mr. and Mrs. Seller that the decision-maker is there. You will waste your time if you get over there and find that the sellers need Uncle Albert's permission to sell.

Remember, the seller has supplied all the facts about himself and the property. You should only volunteer that you're an investor, and that you plan on buying a house this week. This gives a sense of urgency to your conversation. You are really planning on buying a house this week, and you might casually mention that you are looking at a couple of other deals also. By the way, if you must work through a real estate agent, insist that answers to all the questions are complete.

QUESTIONS TO ASK THE SELLER

Motivation

1. Why are you selling?
2. Where will you live after the house is sold?
3. How soon can you leave?
4. If you don't sell, what will you do?
5. Why do you need cash? (Get an answer.)
6. How long have you owned your home?
7. Can you make the decision to sell alone? Do you need to consult any broker? A family member?

Property

1. Tell me what's wrong with it.
2. How old is the roof?
3. Have you had a recent pest control report?
4. Do you have central heat or air?
5. How's the insulation?
6. How did you arrive at the price? Appraisal?
7. Will it need new carpets soon?

Neighborhood

1. Are there mostly renters or owners in your area?
2. Are there schools nearby? Park? Shopping?
3. How are your neighbors?
4. Are many homes for sale in your neighborhood?
5. How would you rate your neighborhood?

Financial

1. What is the existing financing?
2. Is it a conventional loan? FHA? VA? Cal Vet? Private?
3. What are the terms? Interest rate? Due dates? Payments?
4. Tell me about the motivations of the private lenders.

Flexibility

1. Are you flexible on terms and price? (Try for both.)
2. Would you lease the property back?
3. Could you use a lump sum of cash at some future date?
4. If we come to terms, could we close escrow in six months? One year?
5. Would you take something in trade as part of the price?
6. If you felt secure in getting your money each month, would you sell for no down payment?
7. If you got all cash, how much would you discount the price?
8. Do you have any cash to add to a larger deal?

If the Seller Qualified, Make an Appointment

1. Make an appointment.

2. In the meantime, design solutions.

3. Design alternative transactions, using the no down payment formulas.

4. Plan your approach carefully.

You know who Mr. Motivation is and you know how to find him. It is time to qualify him. Does he meet your requirements? Do the property and financing meet your criteria?

As a budding real estate empire builder, you need to use your time as wisely as you spend your cash. Time is money in this business. You will need to develop organized techniques for all facets of your program. Here is a technique that will allow you to contact and qualify sellers from your own home using the telephone.

PREPARING FOR NEGOTIATION

1. After reviewing the seller's answers, you might brainstorm all the facts, impressions, and thoughts you gathered during the phone conversation on a single sheet of paper. Something like this: Will carry financing, doesn't need all cash, daughter going to college in the fall, needs some tuition money, retirement planned in three years, assumable loan, property in nice area, property vacant, needs some repair. Seller has some cash saved.

2. After brainstorming, try to clearly define the seller's problems. The seller's problem is that he is receiving no rent to service his monthly payment. He wants out of the negative cash flow.

3. What does he need? He needs out of the negative cash flow, with possibly a little cash to pay his daughter's tuition. But he does have cash in the bank!

4. Draft alternative preliminary offers. These offers should be tailored to solve the seller's problems and at the same time give you a super real estate deal. Plan your approach with the seller carefully.

5. *Remember that when drafting your offers, the cardinal investment rule of a real estate empire builder is: Buy only at a profit.* I have a friend who insists that he doesn't buy unless he makes one hundred percent on his cash invested going into the deal. This also is a good safety margin in case the market slumps for an extended period.

In your preliminary offers, make sure that you have clearly written down your highest price and the best terms you will give. Don't deviate from your plan.

I have a friend named Charley who used the "telephone questioning technique" recently. He eventually got two super deals in one week for his efforts. Of course, he walked away from the other deals. I asked him how he did so well. He said, "I decided on my top price and terms before I went in to meet the seller and I would not go $1 above the prepared price."

He went on to say that there are enough good deals out there; he doesn't worry about losing one or two deals. The important thing is that the only way you are going to get rich and stay rich is to stick to your guns. Make no exceptions. Stick to that top price and best terms you'll give. In this market, with a little effort, you should be able to get exactly what you want, on your price and terms.

DESIGNING THE PRELIMINARY OFFER

One major mistake a novice real estate investor makes is not bargaining hard enough for the little things in a transaction. The little things might include one percent higher on the interest rate on the note that the seller is carrying back; a shorter due date on the seller carryback note; who's paying the closing costs, etc. The novice thinks, "I've got my price, that's all I am concerned about." Wrong! To be a successful empire builder, you need to fight for every item in the contract. All items are negotiable. For example, a one percent higher interest rate could mean a hundred dollars a month increase in the payment on a

$100,000 mortgage. If you give on a little item such as the closing date, attempt to get a more major item in the transaction, such as a lower interest rate. Generally, you should try to trade off cash-now items in a transaction for future-cash items. Try to always delay cash payments as long as possible into the future.

Let's examine some important negotiable points you should be taking into consideration prior to making an offer.

Negotiable Points in a Transaction

- Price. At times you will be able to pay a higher price with more lenient terms. Be quick to take advantage of this trade-off if it is to your benefit. (I'll show you how to do this in a later chapter.)

- Owner financing. This is where you can really gain an advantage in the negotiating process (see the chapter "Engineering Notes for Maximum Profits").

- Interest rate

- Term, balloon, bubbles (little balloons)

- Monthly payment, annual, no payments

- Moratorium on payments, e.g., until income-tax-refund time, beginning of loan

- Seasonal payments

- Prepayment discount clause

- Substitution of collateral clause

- Performance mortgage

- Subordination clause

- Backdoor clause

- Negative wrap-around

- Wrap-around mortgage (all-inclusive trust deed)

- Ownership and control

- Partnership
- Option
- Lease with an option
- Long escrow
- Life estates
- Down payment
- Cash. How much? When (deferred?), discounts
- Who pays closing costs, pest control, points, prorations?
- When do we close? Liquidated damages?
- Impounds
- Last month's rent, security deposit
- Trade in lieu of cash downs (personal, real, service)
- Note (personal, secured) downs
- Work credit
- You get new loan
- Share the wealth (win-win partnership with seller)
- Assume your obligations, problems
- Earnest money, how much, personal note, postdated check or draft
- Existing financing
- You buy down or seller buys down
- Pay off loan
- Subject to, assumption
- Due on sale
- Shared appreciation mortgage
- Private
  - Definancing

- • Up interest, lower interest
- • Subordinate
- • Trade out
- • Backdoors

- ▪ Weasel clauses

- ▪ Moratorium on payments
  - • New advance
  - • Change term

- ▪ Property

- ▪ The seller will fix, paint, landscape, carpet prior to close of escrow

As this book progresses, you are going to learn how to effectively use these negotiable points—how to combine these items so that you will always buy at a profit. You have determined that this guy is Mr. Motivation and that the property, financing, and neighborhood fit your picture. It's time to do it!

CHAPTER 6
Buying at a Profit: Step II of Negotiations

You are now ready to meet with the seller. You have had time to plan your strategies, draft your preliminary offers, and get prepared. (All success is structured in good preparation!) But you still don't have a deal. In fact, you have not even seen the property.

Before going to meet with the seller, make sure that you have all the items you will need to make the deal on the spot. The following items are helpful, but not always necessary. You will have to determine the appropriateness of each item depending on your particular deal and your level of competence.

BUYER'S TOOLS

- Purchase contract (deposit receipts)
- Checkbook, bank and money market drafts
- Promissory note blank forms
- Business cards
- Your financial statement with references (addresses and phone numbers)
- Option forms
- Lease forms
- Exchange forms
- Pictures of possible trade items (cars, boats, houses)
- Loan amortization book
- Calculator (preferably financial)
- Names, addresses, and phone numbers of notaries nearby
- A newspaper with ads circled (this will show the seller that you are looking at other properties)
- Pencils, pen, notebook (I like a 9 × 12 legal pad).

Dress neatly! You don't need a three-piece suit! That might really intimidate the seller. He may not let you in the door. Of course, this varies with your particular locale. In California, clean slacks and an open neck sports shirt or blouse is adequate, depending on your gender or persuasion.

Your first step, once in the seller's house, is to subtly lower the seller's expectations of profit. You do this by walking around the house and jotting notes in big bold print (you want the seller to see your notes). List any defect you find; for example:

- Needs living room painted

- Needs new carpeting

- Bathroom smells. Must need new floor or new owners!

Put stars next to these items, or underline them. Draw attention to the deficiencies. Also, while going through the house, ask questions that tend to highlight the *negative* aspects of the structure. For instance:

- "Have you checked for dry rot lately in your bathroom?"

- "How long have you been trying to sell?" (Let them know that they need you to solve their problems.)

- "I'll bet maintenance costs you a fortune on this house."

- As you sniff about, you might ask, "Do you have animals?"

Be tactful as you point out the negative aspects of the seller's house. Well-planned, creative questioning is fundamental to your taking control of the direction of negotiations. Create doubt in the seller's mind regarding his price. He might think, "Maybe I am asking too much. Gee, I didn't notice the dry rot in the bathroom."

Making the seller more realistic about his price is the first step of buying at a profit. Also, if you do not want the house, it will still help the seller. He'll be in a better position to determine whether or not he should lower his price and soften his terms.

Create a sense of urgency by using some of the following comments:

- "I'm going to buy a house this week."
- "I'm looking at several other properties."

You might look at your watch frequently. Let the seller know that you mean business—you are not a shopper, you are a buyer! At the same time, act disinterested in the seller's property as you pass through.

Your second step will involve getting everybody seated. Try to steer Mr. and Mrs. Seller toward the kitchen table. Encyclopedia salesmen are taught that most family business is done in the kitchen.

Once you are all seated, make sure that your notebook with all the defects in the house written down is clearly visible. Ask some of the questions that you had asked previously. Psychologists teach us that you have to ask the same question many times to get at the real answer. You might again ask, "Why are you selling?" "What will you do if you don't sell?" Well-planned, creative questioning is fundamental to controlling the direction negotiations take.

If these and other answers correspond to their previous answers, you should feel comfortable in proceeding. If it appears that the seller's motivation has changed, then listen very carefully. You might have to adopt another set of offers. If you are experienced and can digest the new facts and can draft new alternative plans mentally, then by all means hang in there to make the deal right then. For the inexperienced investor, it might be a good idea to leave for a while so that you can digest the new set of facts and how they will affect the deal. It'll be easier to draft a new set of alternatives if you aren't exposed to the pressures of negotiation.

FORMAL NEGOTIATIONS BEGIN

"If I were willing to commit to a deal tonight, what is the rock-bottom price you would accept?"

The number that the seller mentions will give you the highest price you will pay. It establishes the upper limit in the negotiating range. If the seller counters your question with a question such as, "What is the price you would be willing to pay?" be noncommittal! Make the seller commit to a price and you will control the direction of the negotiations.

One technique that is used after asking, "What is the lowest price you will accept?" is to be silent! Silence is a potent negotiating tool.

The seller might say, "$65,000." Keep silent and stare at him. He might say, "Well, my absolute rock-bottom price is $63,000, that's it." Keep silent. Do you get the idea? As Chesterton said, "Silence is the unbeatable repartee."

At this point, you might write down a price on a legal pad and say, "This is the highest I think I can go, *under the circumstances.*" Emphasize the word *circumstances* and point to your notebook with all the negative aspects of the property listed. If you get a lot of flack, tactfully review the negative aspects of the house; also mention that you are going to look at other properties tonight.

If you hit a price roadblock, start working on terms. Many times you can pay the owner more than he or she is asking, if easy terms are given. A seller is much more likely to give you a longer term on the note than lower the price. Generally, each year you add to the note lowers the price of the property. (We will talk about this in a later chapter.)

Once there appears to be acceptance of the price and terms, pencil it out neatly on a legal pad or notebook. Make it clear and in a logical sequence.

When everybody is satisfied, it is time to fill in the legal contract. Up until now, it has just been talk. It is time to nail down the deal with a legally binding contract. In California, we use the deposit receipt to legally bind the deal.

THE PURCHASE CONTRACT

Follow these rules when filling out the real estate purchase contract:

1. Name the buyer. Put John Smith (your name) or his assignees. This gives you added flexibility. It allows you to legally resell the property prior to the closing date. If just your name is on the contract, a remorseful seller might stand in the way of you and a quick profit.

2. Earnest money. The seller wants the maximum amount of earnest money or deposit. He figures that if he is going to take his property off the market for an extended period of time, he wants a solid sale. The real estate empire builder, always mindful of the Conservation of Cash Philosophy, wants to limit his cash deposit. One dollar is deemed legal by the law. However, very few sellers will accept one dollar as a deposit. However, they might accept any of the following:

- Personal (promissory) note to be redeemed at the close of escrow by either cash or other secured property

- A postdated check to be redeemed at the close of escrow

- Bank draft redeemable at the close of escrow

- Money market draft redeemable at the close of escrow

- A check for $100, if you have the money

- Personal property as consideration, i.e., pink slip to a car

Here is a place where your ability to substitute ideas for cash really comes in handy. *Minimize all cash outlays when making an offer.* You will run out of cash quickly if you go around putting $500 deposits on a lot of properties. You could have thousands of dollars floating between deals and tied up for extended periods of time waiting for escrow to close. Being a real estate empire builder means always keeping maximum control of your cash.

Try to always give the deposit money to a title company or a third party acting as escrow agent for the transaction.

3. When you close is very important. In inflationary times, we are betting that the longer we control a promising real estate investment, the more money we will make. If we can lock in today's price for, let's say, a one-year escrow, we have succeeded in controlling the greatest appreciating investment today, without the associated holding costs. Try to get sixty- to ninety-day escrows. The longer, the better.

Also, by carefully designing your closing date to correspond with the rent due date, you will be able to collect a full month's rent in advance of your first payment, which is usually thirty days after the close of escrow. (We will go into details of how this works in a later chapter.)

When you delay a close, it gives you a chance to raise the cash that might be needed to close escrow through such methods as applying for a loan, getting a partner, etc.

4. The weasel clauses can help you out of binds and ensure you maximum flexibility. The weasel clause is also called a contingency clause or "subject to" clause. Let's look at some weasel clauses.

- This offer is contingent upon buyer reviewing a standard pest control report and approving it within a ten-day period.

- This offer is contingent upon the buyer applying for and receiving a thirty-year FHA loan of $65,000, not exceeding twelve percent interest.

- This offer is contingent upon the approval of the buyer's partner within a ten-day period. (You may not have a partner, but you now have ten days to find one. I have used this clause successfully many times in my offers.)

Real estate agents do not like weasel clauses. They want the deal pinned down so that they can be certain about getting that commission.

- Weasel clauses give you a cooling-off period. You might make a hasty deal only to see that a costly error was made in entering into the transaction. If it was not a good deal, use your weasel clause to back out.

- Weasel clauses give you time to raise any cash down payment you might need.

- Weasel clauses protect you if new information about the property is received, such as that there is extensive termite damage.

One well-written weasel clause will be a lot more effective than five or six. If you complicate the deal by asking for too many contingencies, the seller is liable to back off. I had this happen to me when I was young and knew it all. Just like the old saying, "It ain't the things you don't know what gets you into trouble, it's the things you know for sure what just ain't so." I thought I knew too much!

FINAL PHASE OF NEGOTIATION

Some final points about negotiation. If you have clearly come upon a super deal, do not squabble over minor points. Wrap the deal up as fast as you can. I have seen super deals lost because the buyer was trying to get an additional $1,000 off the price and somebody else stepped right in and gave the seller what he wanted. How can you know if it is a super deal? Knowledge! *Get to thoroughly know the market!*

If your negotiations bog down, always leave an offer with the seller. Specify that he has twenty-four hours to accept it. If you don't get the deal accepted, take heart. There will be others. Most successful investors say real estate is a numbers game. You have got to make a lot of offers and get involved in many negotiations to yield one profitable deal. But when you get that deal and you see that you have made $10,000 going into the transaction, you will have clearly learned an important lesson as a real estate empire builder. But only at a profit!

CHAPTER 7
Pulling Money Out of a Hat

The central theme of this book is to teach you how to acquire as much property as you can without using any of your own money. To build a real estate empire starting from scratch requires that you become extremely resourceful. You need to *substitute ideas for cash*.

We are all well aware of the cash that we have in the bank. We know that it is a limited commodity, a vanishing breed in today's economy. Cash is king! We have got to learn to stretch each real and potential dollar of ours so that it becomes an investment dollar, not a consumer dollar. Investment dollars will compound themselves to great wealth, if properly used. Consumer dollars are gone—they disappear. That wealth will never be recovered.

For instance, if Joe Consumer were to receive a cash gift of, say, $1,000, how do you suppose he would use it? He would probably spend it! Right? On a new car (or slightly used one at today's prices), a hot boat, a Caribbean cruise—or money would just slip away over a period of time on nonessential gadgets and toys.

The empire builder, on the other hand, practices the Conservation of Cash Philosophy. Spend your vanishing cash only on essentials and investments that will grow in value, such as a nice real estate investment. An appreciating real estate investment is like a money farm in today's world. It grows a new crop each year. On the other hand, the car that you bought five years ago is beginning to fall apart; your hard-earned money is disappearing before your very eyes.

In this chapter, I am going to give you some simple ideas successful real estate empire builders have used to get started. These formulas are only a beginning. The combinations and variations from these basic formulas could run into the thousands. It all depends upon the unique transaction in which you wish to use them.

My suggestion is that, as you read through the no down payment formulas, have a pen and paper handy and jot down variations, combinations, and the applications to those deals in which you are involved or would like to be involved.

Let's now look at some ways in which you can raise a cash down payment starting with nothing.

Formula #1   The Family Connection

Make a written list of all family members, friends, acquaintances, and friends of friends from whom you might be able to borrow cash. List people who know of your integrity (unless you don't have any, in which case you had better begin building it quickly. The novice empire builder won't get very far if he doesn't keep his word. Honesty first!).

List people who know you, but who need additional incentives to loan you money, such as sharing potential profits in the property, a high interest rate, etc. Most young homeowners today have used this technique for their first purchase. I did!

Formula #2   Unlocking the Insurance Safe

Borrow against your life insurance policy. Most whole life insurance policies allow you to borrow against them. The interest rate you will be charged is generally substantially below the prevailing market rate. Let's say that you borrow from your insurance policy and have to pay an eight percent interest rate. Does that sound ridiculous? Check on your own policy. I think you will be surprised at how cheap it is. Using the principle of *creative debt*, we might expect to make at least thirty percent per year on a good real estate investment, and we pay eight percent. That is a twenty-two percent net gain. Not too bad! Actually, if you know what you are doing, you can make that yield in your sleep in real estate. I have rarely made less than one hundred percent on borrowed money.

Formula #3   Cash In Your Life Insurance

Cash in your existing whole life insurance policy. You can generally cover your insurance needs by taking out a term policy, and it will probably cost you less, too. Most life insurance policies with a cash value have ridiculously low yields. The insured gets ripped off. The insurance companies use this cheap source of money to invest . . . where? In real estate, of course, making much higher yields than they are paying out. The insurance companies understand the magic of going into creative debt to get rich. Cash in your policy so that you can reap the rewards of creative debt.

Formula #4   Family Syndicate

Form a small syndication of family or friends to raise cash. A syndication is a group of people who get together for a specific purpose, in this case for a real estate investment. If you need $5,000 for a down payment on a super deal, and cannot raise it from one family member or friend, try this: Get ten of your friends to loan you $500 each. This would be a type of small, informal syndication. Under these circumstances, it would be best to borrow the money using your personal note.

If you try to give ten people a small ownership interest in your first purchase, you will regret it the rest of your life. Trying to satisfy ten people's unique desires, opinions, and investment needs will have you running in circles and wasting valuable time.

Formula #5   Finance Companies

Try approaching your local finance company for an unsecured loan. If you have a secure job and a good credit history, your local Benevolent Financial Inc. can probably help. These loans can be very expensive. An unsecured loan through a finance company might carry an interest rate as high as thirty percent. Before tapping high-cost sources, of course, be sure that you have a great buy and that you have adequate monthly income to service the payments.

If your credit is the pits or you have no credit history, you might try using a cosigner. A way of lowering the cost of this loan would be to secure it with a piece of real estate, either yours, a family member's, or a friend's.

Formula #6   Mail Order Money

Mail order finance companies might be an alternative source of funds, particularly if you are trying to maintain a low-profile investor image. You will find these companies advertising in *The Wall Street Journal*, *Money Magazine*, *Fortune*, etc. These companies cater to executives, lawyers, doctors, and other professional people.

Formula #7   Credit Union

Do you, or members of your family, belong to a credit union? If so, this is a great source of cash. These loans are fairly easy to get, and normally the cost is fairly reasonable. Credit unions usually try to get an added touch of security by being able to deduct monthly payments from your regular paycheck. If you are not a member of a credit union, perhaps your spouse or a parent is. Most credit unions allow family members lending privileges if they, too, join.

If you would like to lower the amount of interest charged, try having the loan secured by a savings account in the credit union. This is called a compensating balance. Remember, the money in the savings account does not have to be yours. It might be your parent's account, or someone else's money in your account.

On the second purchase that I made, I borrowed $1,500 from a credit union. At the time, I was nervous about going into deeper debt, but after reviewing all the facts, I said, "Go for it." In a couple of months, I sold the property for a $2,000 profit. Wasn't bad for about ten hours work. That is using creative debt, investing borrowed funds to create wealth. My only mistake was that I sold it. To build a real estate empire, you need to buy and hold!

Formula #8   Employer Advance

Your employer might advance you funds for that first down payment. He could deduct a specific monthly payment each month to repay the advance. This program might be offered as an employee's incentive plan. A lot of larger companies have been giving these types of advances to promising employees in recent years.

A variation on this formula might work like this: Your employer buys the house and you lease it back with an option to purchase. He gets the tax benefits of ownership through the depreciation expense. You get a home sweet home and the potential appreciation benefits the option offers. (See the chapter on options. I will go through how to structure such a transaction.)

Formula #9   Advertise for Cash

Place an ad in your local newspaper under the "Money Wanted" or "Financial Investments" column asking to borrow money unsecured. You will have to offer a high interest rate, and you might have to give the lender a share in your future profits. If you get a response and the prospective lender appears to balk at a commitment, offer to secure the note with the property you are about to buy. Be creative! Give the money man incentives that he cannot refuse. (Warning: You might get a friendly call from your local loan shark. Stay away from this guy! It is not worth it!)

Formula #10   Inheritance

Do you have an inheritance, a trust, or a gift expected at a future date? The seller might be willing to accept your personal note secured contractually by one of these sources.

I have a friend whose name is John. He received an inheritance. The only trouble was that the money was in a trust and could not be touched for five years. John is a creative real estate empire builder. The money was certain to come, so John made offers to unlock his future wealth and use it now. He created a promissory note secured by the trust.

There are companies who will buy your right to an inheritance or trust. You will probably have to take a steep discount, but these people pay cash in today's dollars. Many of the so-called trusts that people have are being managed by conservative bankers. They don't generally conserve capital in our inflationary times. They are losing purchasing power daily. Many trusts are achieving negative yields after inflation is considered. If you can use your money today by putting it in good solid real estate investments, you will be taking a much more sensible conservation of capital strategy.

If you are expecting an inheritance from a living relative or friend, it might be good to easily point out the financial benefits of gifts versus inheritances. Consult an attorney or do some reading on estate planning before you make your presentation.

If you have any future payments owed to you such as job bonus, balloon payments on notes, gifts, insurance settlements, I.R.S. refunds, lawsuit payoffs, consider pledging these future payments instead of a cash down payment.

Formula #11 Personal Note

Give the seller your own personal or promissory note as a down payment. A personal note (also known as a promissory note) is just an I.O.U. You are deferring, not eliminating, the time you might have to come up with cash. You will either defer that cash by paying it off monthly, or you might just pay interest only and give the seller a balloon payment at the end of a particular period, such as one or two years.

If you do not pay the note, the seller cannot look to the property as security. He has to legally go after your personal assets.

I have given personal notes to sellers, and I have taken them in lieu of cash. The biggest danger in taking an unsecured note is bankruptcy of the maker. If the maker goes under, the holder of the note might get wiped out. If you give a personal note and something goes sour, you could have a lien placed against all your property, personal and real. The personal note unlocks one of the most important of your hidden assets, your ability to convince the seller that you are a trustworthy and responsible individual. Use it, don't abuse it.

INCENTIVES THE LENDER MIGHT LIKE

Let's now take a look at the various incentives you might offer a lender for additional security.

1. Convince him of your creditworthiness
   - references
   - financial statement
   - credit check

2. Get a cosigner
   - parent, friend
   - pay a cosigner

3. Pay higher than market interest rate

4. Pay higher than market monthly payments

5. Shortern the length of repayment

6. Raise the price of the real estate

7. You get option to buy, lender gets ownership and tax benefits

8. Partnership

9. Share some of the appreciation with the lender

10. Give the lender a year's worth of postdated checks

The basic philosophy of *No Down Payment Formulas* is simply, "Money flows toward ideas." You don't need to have a dime in your bank account to buy real estate. You do need to know how to structure and arrange ideas so that the necessary cash to complete a transaction will be there.

By choosing the right piece of property and by designing attractive incentive packages for investors and lenders, you'll be able to buy without ever using any of your own cash. Your friendly lenders and investors will win and you will win by "harnessing" the great appreciation benefits of real estate.

When a loan is due, pay it off a day or two early in the beginning stages. As the lender gains more confidence in your trustworthiness, a more flexible repayment attitude may be taken.

Keep your friendly banker informed. Get to know him personally. Try to find a legitimate reason to talk to him each time you go into the bank. Let him know of your successes. "Gee, you know, Mr. Banker, just last week I sold a piece of property and made $25,000 on it." Mr. Banker likes to see you get liquid once in a while. It helps him sleep better! It doesn't hurt to make large deposits in your account periodically, even if it's just with borrowed money. All this is designed to build an image of financial solidity around you. Also, ask for more money each time you go back. Your success record will grow with your banker's increased confidence in your abilities.

Formula #12   Bank Round Robin

One technique widely used to establish unsecured credit includes the use of several banks. Commercial loans are well suited for using this formula. It goes like this: You open a checking account at a local bank. If you have good credit and already have a checking account, stay put at your bank. If your credit stinks with the bank in which you have a checking account, it is time to change. Close your account and get a fresh start with another bank.

Put $500 in your new checking account. Borrow it, if you need to, from a friend or family member. Wait a few days, and then go to your newfound banker and request an unsecured loan for $500 for one month. You indicate to him that you are a real estate investor, a real Mr. Businessman, and that you want to build a good credit rating with him. In fact, let him know that if he is the least bit uncertain about repayment, you will leave $500 in your checking account until the loan is repaid. Mr. Banker should like that and will probably grant you the loan without hesitation.

You then take the $500 from the loan proceeds and open a checking account at another bank. You then repeat the unsecured loan request. If you repeat this technique ten times, you have just established a $5,000 unsecured line of credit. The magic of this formula is that you can use it even if you have poor credit, or no credit history.

How do you pay Mr. Banker back? You could repay with borrowed money by repeating this process over a staggered time period (for example, one loan might be

due in one month from May 1, and you arrange to have
another loan funded on June 1 to pay off the May 1 loan.
Theoretically, you might never have to pay the principal
off. You would only have to service the interest payments). Other methods of repayment would include selling some of your real estate, improving the property to a
point where you could refinance the property to pay off
your short-term debt, or roll over your debts from banks
to friends to family back to banks. Your own ability to
create solutions is the only limit you will find.

Be sure and pay off Mr. Banker on time. If you do, next
time you might get a $1,000 loan, then $5,000, etc. The line
of credit will be an important tool for you to expand your
empire rapidly. Start today!

Formula #13   The Plastic Crank

Did you know that there is an unsecured line of credit
built into your plastic credit cards such as MasterCard, Visa,
American Express, etc.? With minimal credit requirements,
you obtain credit cards from many different banks in your
area. Most banks offer two different credit cards. Let's say
that there are twenty-five banks in your area. That gives
you a chance of obtaining fifty credit cards. Most banks
will give you cash advances on each of your cards. Generally, your initial limit might be $500 per card, unless, of
course, you have a good credit history; then you might get
up to $2,500 or more. With fifty cards at $500 per card, that
could give you a $25,000 line of credit. That is a lot of
down payment money to begin to fuel your empire.

This is expensive credit, so again, make sure that your
creative debt strategy is sound. Have alternative repayment plans in case something goes wrong. Be prepared
for the unexpected and you will never have to worry!

Formula #14   S & L Credit Cards

Savings and loans have recently instituted their own
credit cards, although most of them require that you leave
cash in your savings account equal to the amount of your
credit limit. For example, let's say that you have decided

to charge some building materials to be used on a promising fixer-upper you just acquired. The building materials came to $1,000. That means that the savings and loan company wants you to keep $1,000 frozen in a savings account. This is called a compensating balance.

You might get a friend to deposit the required funds in your savings account. Give your friend an incentive if necessary, such as an interest bonus. The future of these advances might bring lower compensating balances. Call around and find out what the requirements are in your area.

Formula #15   Home Improvement Loan

Banks and savings and loan companies both offer home improvement loans, sometimes with up to fifteen-year payback terms. If you don't own property, or if your credit is the pits, perhaps a family member might loan his or her house as security. The family member actually gets the loan. Your responsibility would be to make the monthly payments. Remember, design incentives so that you will benefit and the person with security will benefit.

Formula #16   Compensating Balances

Compensating balances allow Mr. Banker to sleep better at night. A compensating balance is an amount of money left in a savings or checking account as security for a loan. If you don't have the spare cash, get a friend to place money in your savings account, just as he might do in the savings and loan example. Also, there are lenders who, for an interest premium, would be glad to have their funds used for a compensating balance. I have seen ads for these types of loans in *The Wall Street Journal*, *Money Magazine*, *Fortune*, etc.

Remember, the empire builder gives the lender whatever security is necessary to ensure that he has a dependable source of cash. Having a dependable source of cash allows you to take advantage of super deals quickly.

Formula #17   Personal Property Loans

Banks love to make loans on cars, boats, R.V.s, airplanes, etc., or basically any personal property that could be liquidated in case of a default. Mr. Banker might be glad to take the pink slip on your car as security for a loan. These types of loans might be written over a one- to seven-year period.

If your bank is not interested in refinancing some of your personal property, perhaps the local Benevolent Financial Inc. would love to write a loan of this type. This is a great source of generating that cash down payment.

Formula #18   Other Collateralized Loans

Stocks and bonds normally are acceptable collateral for Mr. or Mrs. Banker. You will also find that some banks will lend money using such unconventional collateral as gold, silver, diamonds, artwork, or fine gemstones. Again, if you do not have any of these items, consider borrowing your collateral.

Formula #19   Refinance Cash

Banks and savings and loans are in the business of arranging long-term loans secured by real estate. When interest rates are at a reasonable level, these money merchants are an excellent source for refinancing cash out of existing property, and thus harvesting the growth in your equity. Remember, growth in equity can occur in any or all of the following:

1. Time appreciation

2. Buying under market value

3. Creating value by fix-up work

4. Paying down the mortgage.

One way in which I have used this formula is to buy a house at a discount by paying all cash to the loan. I then refinance all my cash back out of the transaction after the close of escrow. For example, several years ago I bought a three-bedroom, two-bath tract home. I paid $30,000 for it, which was well under market value, and gave the seller $3,000 cash to the existing loans. Upon close of escrow, I applied to Happy Savings and Loan for a new loan of slightly over $30,000. The loan was granted for the full amount. The net result was that I was able to acquire my own home using other people's money—a nice nothing down transaction.

Why did I wait until acquiring title before placing the new loan on the property? Lenders are reluctant to loan you one hundred percent of the purchase price of a property, even if the appraisal far exceeds the price. However, once you take title to the property, most lenders will rely on the appraisal as the primary basis for making a loan. In the above example, the appraisal on the property stated a $40,000 value. A $30,000 loan constituted a seventy-five percent loan-to-value ratio and, as such, was a very safe loan from the lender's perspective. The key to making this transaction work was finding Mr. and Mrs. Motivation. Once you've found flexible sellers, your probability of making a nothing down deal will be greatly enhanced. By the way, when we refinance properties that we own, any cash received by ourselves is considered tax-free. Borrowed money is exempt from taxes.

Formula #20   *Loan Brokers*

Loan brokers are an excellent source of secondary money. But they are expensive. Points—that is, the commission fee paid for placing the loan—can be up to twenty percent of the loan. And, the interest rate is generally three or four percentage points above the T-bill rate.

Loan brokers, or equity lenders as they are sometimes called, normally are not very concerned about your credit rating. Their primary concern is the equity cushion in the property on which they might place a loan. They will usually place up to an eighty percent loan on a property in relation to its value. That is, on a $100,000 house a loan broker might consider an $80,000 loan.

If you do not have your own property with sufficient

equity, innovate! You should have begun to get the creative flair of an empire builder by now.

Remember, the creative application of your ideas is your most valuable asset. Use other people's money to make money. Structure, organize, combine, synthesize the ideas necessary to have all the cash you want coming your way. The ideas in the previous two chapters are only a starting point. Expand on them; tailor them to solve the initial cash problems you might have to make that first super buy. Start today!

CHAPTER 8
Substituting Barter for Cash

Barter is as old as mankind itself! From the very beginning we've exchanged that which we had in surplus for that which we needed. "I'll trade you my wheat for your corn." Why would I make such a trade? Because I need corn and you need the wheat. All business enterprises are based on fulfilling the needs of people.

A real estate empire builder understands this process very well. He makes his fortune by solving problems and thus fulfilling needs. The more real estate problems you solve, the more money you'll make.

Barter generally does not involve the use of money. Money is only a medium of exchange, a storehouse of wealth. The real purpose of money is to use it to obtain what you need. In *No Down Payment Formulas*, I am trying to give you ideas as substitutes for the cash that a seller might require.

Find out what the seller needs! When the seller says, "I need cash," try to discover how he is going to spend it. Probe deeply into the seller's motivations and you will find what is needed. He might need to pay off some bills, buy a new car, take a trip to Hawaii, or just a steady source of additional income. With a little creativity, you should be able to give the seller what he wants without spending any cash.

Let's see how the magic of barter will help you create your real estate empire substituting commodities and services for cash.

Formula #21   Substitute Needs for Cash

Recently, my friend John stopped by to discuss a particular real estate problem. He was very excited about a nice rental house. He explained, "The house is well located, with good renters, and the price is well below market. Ed, he is only asking $50,000 and I know the market value of homes in that area is at least $60,000." He went on to say, "There is only one problem."

"What's that?" I asked.

"The seller needs all cash for his equity. I need $10,000, fast! I am all tapped out on my line of credit at the bank. What do you think I should do?"

I said, "Find out why the seller needs $10,000." After some discussion, John went back to the seller.

I got a call a couple of days later from John. As it turned out, John discovered that the seller needed money to buy lumber. He needed the lumber to finish building his new house.

John identified the need. Being an aggressive real estate empire builder, he was determined to fill that need. John found a lumber company that would extend him credit for ninety days. John bought the lumber for Mr. Seller. He traded the lumber for the entire equity in the nice rental house.

Within ninety days John had arranged for a second mortgage from his bank, secured by the house. He used this money to pay off the lumber company. How was John able to do this? He bought the house so far under market value that there was plenty of equity available to secure a new second mortgage.

Mr. Seller was happy, he got the lumber for his new home and out of rental management. And John was happy! He got a nice house in a growing neighborhood without using any money out of his pocket. A sweet no down payment deal for John. Opportunity knocked for John because he was willing to search for a solution that gave him that super deal.

Formula #22   Assume Debts

Through some creative questioning and listening, find out if the seller has any pressing debts. Find out if you can assume these obligations. Try to transfer his or her credit card obligations over to your credit cards. Generally a credit card company will be cooperative in getting these debts transferred, particularly if you have good credit. If the debts include a car loan, discuss with Mr. Seller's banker transferring the loan to your car. Try to defer payment whenever possible. Before taking on Mr. Seller's debts, make sure that you are getting some healthy concessions on the price and terms. Also, make sure that you can handle the monthly payments, or very soon you will find yourself snowed under with debt obligations.

Formula #23   The S & L Problem Solver

If you come upon a seller who is in foreclosure, find out who the beneficiary is; if it is a savings and loan with a credit card operation, you might have an opportunity to put the back payments on a credit card. You have solved the seller's big problem. He should be agreeable to taking a flexible note for the remainder of his equity. Remember,

Formula #21:   Substitute Needs for Cash

REAL ESTATE PURCHASE AGREEMENT
AND RECEIPT FOR DEPOSIT

This is intended to be a legally binding contract. Read it carefully.

_____ , _____ , 19 ____
_____(City)_____   _(State)_

Received from _____ ,
                              (Name)
herein called Buyer, the sum of ___ one hundred _____
_____ dollars $ _100.00_ , in the form of cash ☐ ,
cashier's check ☐ personal check ☐ or ___ promissory note ___ ☒ payable to
                    (Name)   , to be held uncashed
until acceptance of this offer, as deposit on account of purchase price of _____
___ fifty thousand _____ dollars $ _50,000.00_
for the purchase of property located in _____ ,
                                               (City)
County of _____ , _____ ,
            (County)   _(State)_
described as follows: _____
                         (Address or other legal description)
_____

Buyer will deposit in escrow with _____
                                   (Title company or other third party)
the balance of purchase price as follows: _____

___ 1.   Seller to accept $10,000 worth of credit at lumber yard
___   as $10,000 down payment.

___ 2.   Buyer to assume existing $40,000 loan.

_____
_____
_____
_____
_____
_____
_____
_____
_____
_____
_____
_____
_____
_____
_____
_____
_____

Detail above any factual terms and conditions applicable to this sale, such as financing, contingency of sale of other property, the disposition of structural pest control inspection, and repairs and personal property to be included in the sale.

Deposit will ☐ will not ☐ be increased by $ _____ to $ _____
within _____ days of acceptance of this offer.

Buyer does ☐ does not ☐ intend to occupy subject property as his residence.

The supplements initialed below are incorporated as part of this agreement.

____ Structural Pest Control Certification Agreement   ____ VA Amendment
____ Special Studies Zone Disclosure   ____ FHA Amendment
____ Flood Insurance Disclosure   ____ Other _____
____ Occupancy Agreement   ____ Other _____

Buyer and Seller acknowledge receipt of a copy of this page, which constitutes page 1 of _____ Pages.

X _____   X _____
   Buyer   Seller
X _____   X _____
   Buyer   Seller

you will never know if the savings and loan will let you do this unless you ask.

This technique is just a different application of substituting needs for cash and assuming the seller's debts. It's a good example of how we can take one or two ideas and creatively apply them in many different situations.

Formula #24 Buy or Lease the Seller a Dream

During negotiations, ask if the seller has ever wanted to go on an exotic vacation like Hawaii, a Caribbean cruise, a trip to Europe . . . or you might ask, "If you could have any car of your choice, what would you choose?"

Let Mr. and Mrs. Seller talk. Listen carefully. After you have discovered their dream, give it to them at full retail price. The dream is used instead of a cash down payment. Shop around and try to put the dream on your credit card or an installment plan. Try to trade something you have to obtain the seller's dream. Try to acquire it on credit terms at less than retail value. Then trade it at retail to the seller.

A lot of people see their real estate equities as a direct means to future dreams. Give it to them and you have fulfilled a need. Other dream items might include airplanes, boats, R.V.s—in trader jargon these items are called toys. You can use toys as incentives for lenders, for partners, or for options. Use this motivation in the consumer man and woman and you will be rich soon.

Formula # 25 Sweat Equity

Trade your skills and abilities as a down payment. An attorney may be able to supply legal services; an accountant, tax preparations; a contractor, building skills; a business consultant, a bit of advice; etc.

Evaluate what saleable skills you have. Below is a partial list of tradeable skills in the marketplace today. Which are yours? Add some other skills!

sheetrock	TV repair
upholstery	travel agent
carpenter	mortician

plumber	masseur, masseuse
auto mechanic	"hard worker"
heating/air conditioning	secretary
roofer	contractor
electrician	property manager
landscaper	tutor
appraiser	business consultant
real estate investor	doctor
tiles	pilot
carpet layer	taxidermy
mason	public relations
well driller	ad writing

Everyone has particular services that need to be accomplished—personal and business. Perform services for people and their cash needs are considerably reduced or eliminated—and so will yours be.

I know a lady who traded a year of her secretarial skills as a down payment on a house. The person with whom she traded is an accomplished empire builder. There will come a point in your real estate acquisition program when you will need someone to look out for the detail work. You might consider trading a house equity for secretarial time. Remember the Conservation of Cash Philosophy. Spending cash is only a last resort; barter for your needs.

What about that fixer-upper house? You don't have the spare cash to perform the necessary repairs! What do you do? Trade for the labor and materials. Give a partnership interest in the house. Get done what needs to be done without cash.

Formula #26   Pledge Credit Card Use

Pledge the use of a couple of credit cards (by now you should have more than one) to Mr. and Mrs. Seller. You might offer this to them as "mad money"—a night on the town, new clothes, a quick trip to the mountains, or whatever they want. People today generally have a consumer mentality. They want it now! Many people are willing to trade their appreciating real estate for items that will vanish tomorrow.

The prudent seller might not buy the mad money approach. In this case, be more practical. Offer to pay his monthly food bill or gasoline for a specific period, such as one year.

Be sure that any pledges on your part can be fulfilled. Also, be sure to pin down all facts of the trade contractually, such as time period, spending limits, exclusions, and what happens in case of default.

Formula #27 Prepaid Leases

Prepaid leases on houses, apartments, and commercial spaces can provide a great substitute for a cash down payment.

I have a friend named Jack. He had found a Mrs. Motivation. She was in foreclosure, the boat was sinking fast. Still, she insisted on cash for her equity. Jack questioned her further. "Why do you need cash? What are you going to do with it?"

She indicated that she had her eye on a fancy apartment down by the river. Jack, being an accomplished empire builder, went out and located a luxury apartment complex down by the river. It was almost fifty percent vacant. In tough economic times, lots of people who lived high on the hog when money was loose move out of their fancy apartments for more modest rentals. I like the modest rental concept of investment; it is a way of further reducing your risk.

Jack was able to get a one-year prepaid lease on an apartment in the luxury complex. When Mrs. Seller saw the apartment, she liked it. She took the one-year prepaid lease instead of a cash down payment on her house. The rest of the equity was carried back very flexibly by Mrs. Seller.

How did Jack get a one-year prepaid lease on the apartment? Jack traded his ability to manage the property and fill up vacancies for the prepaid lease. Jack combined his skills with giving Mrs. Motivation what she wanted. Everyone got what they wanted. Everybody ends up a winner!

Formula #28   The Two-Way Exchange

In exchange jargon, this is called a two-way exchange. It works like this: You approach a seller who owns a nice piece of real estate in an area in which you would like to buy. The seller remarks, "Yeah, I'm flexible as long as I get enough money to buy another house."

What is Mr. Seller really saying? *He will sell his house if he can get another comparable house.* Find a new house for him! Don't go running around in circles right away. Sit down and ask the seller the following questions, and then listen:

- Where would you like to live?

- What type of neighborhood?

- What kind of monthly payments can you handle?

- Do you have any cash saved to add to a transaction?

- Describe exactly what you are looking for in a house.

Creatively question and listen before you even attempt to find Mr. Seller a house.

Then go out and find Mr. Seller a new property. You've got to find a seller who is motivated and one who has a house Mr. Seller might like. It is a tall order, but it is possible! Try using a good real estate agent. Give him a piece of the action if he's successful.

You acquire Mr. Seller's future house with one of the No Down Payment formulas; then trade it to Mr. Seller for his present house.

You get the house you originally wanted. Mr. Seller gets his house, and Mr. Motivation (new house seller) gets a problem solved.

If Mr. Seller is very unrealistic in his requirements, have him find the house he wants and then attempt to acquire that property. Why do this? You might be working with an inflexible seller or a seller with other considerations. The seller of the new house might be more flexible in his demands. With this technique you will have just shifted attention from an inflexible decision maker to a more flexible one. By doing this you will increase your chances of success.

___

Formula #29 Buy Wholesale, Sell Retail

Buy items for wholesale value and trade them at retail. For example, my friend Steve recently acquired some gemstones at a fraction of their retail appraisal. He was able to trade the gemstones at retail value for houses, land, boats, cars, etc. He could do this for the following reasons:

1. He found motivated sellers.

2. He found people who saw gemstones as an acceptable currency storehouse of wealth in exchange circles.

3. He found people who like the gemstones more than the items they had.

This same technique can be used with diamonds, artwork, closeout merchandise, antiques, estate jewelry, furniture, recreational lots, etc.

Recreational lots are also known as currency land. This type of land is generally not saleable for cash. It might be desert land, landlocked pieces of ground, unbuildable lots, etc. For years, the key to making this idea work was to buy currency land (with borrowed money, of course) wholesale and trade it retail; then creatively solve the problems of the new property. This technique can yield fat profits. Millions have been made by using this technique.

Who would accept such items at obviously inflated prices? I have! I accepted currency items for an apartment building that I owned. These apartments were driving me bananas. I was a classic Mr. Motivation. The building wasn't bad—the tenants just drove me crazy. I had a management problem, and I wanted out.

Management problems can be cured with a little grit, some creativity, or by letting a professional management firm handle your units. Your time can be more productively spent finding new deals.

I accepted currency land for part of my equity and a carryback note from Mr. Problem Solver; did I lose? I took a breather, then went out and found a builder who was overextended. I traded the carryback note received from my apartment building for the builder's brand-new home. The currency land I had taken eventually traded into several rental properties. There are always Mr. Motivations in the marketplace! We all can end up winners!

Formula #30   *The College Carrot*

Find a seller who is planning on sending children to college soon. His motivation for selling might be to raise cash to cover the college costs. If the seller is insistent on cash, since he feels that is the only way he can solve the problem, try following this procedure: Find out what college the seller's children are planning to attend. Go to that school's manager of the endowment fund. Ask him if the school would exchange tuition, room, and board at the college for equity in a nice house. Many schools are attracted to this sort of deal. If the manager agrees, ask him if the school would be willing to sell the house to you for no down payment and carry a note back for the balance of their equity. Colleges like a regular, secure cash flow. Convince the endowment fund manager that the note payments will be on time and be very secure.

After reaching a tentative agreement with the college, go back and arrange to have the seller exchange his property to the college for the future college costs. You then acquire the property for no money down from the college.

Find that knot of anxiety in the seller, relieve it, and you will be rich. Wealth flows to those who help fill a need.

Formula #31   *Life Estates and Cash Flow*

Most retired people are long on available time and short on cash flow. Ninety-five percent of the people in our country retire dependent upon an inadequate pension plan, paltry Social Security payments, or society's charity. Inflation's got retirees by the pursestrings! Here's a plan that can help a young real estate empire builder or an old empire builder make big profits and at the same time help retired folks who own their own home obtain a higher cash flow.

Work out an arrangement to buy the retiree's house for no down payment; however, you might give him monthly payments that would supplement his income. Give him a life estate to the property. That is, you do not get possession until they (if it's a husband and wife) die.

Make sure that you design the offer so that it is mutually beneficial. Have the retirees consult an attorney for advice. You might need to consult an actuary to determine the optimum monthly payments. Should it be quarterly? Annually? There are a lot of older people in our country who don't get enough to eat, yet are sitting on fat real estate equities. This might solve a problem for them. Do your homework on this one—it is good future ground for wealth building.

Formula #32   Creating Wealth

Find a house you can buy for no down payment with a price tag below market. Relax, it can be done! I know that because I have done it. Use that property as a down payment for a seller who is nervous about you not putting cash down on his house. Almost any house with one hundred percent financing has a recognizable exchangeable equity. You'll find this true because of the tax benefits inherent in improved real property ownership, and because the market generally assumes that there is some equity in any property above and beyond the loans.

The seller of the original property will sleep a whole lot better for two reasons:

1. He is getting some consideration as down payment on the sale of the property. He might feel that you have more of a vested interest in not walking away from the property.

2. You have demonstrated that you are not a deadbeat;

after all, you are a real-life property owner. "Must be a solid, stable guy."

With a little imagination, combined with a little effort, you have truly pulled a real estate equity out of a hat.

Formula #33   *Buy at a Discount, Trade Full Value*

Trade Mr. Motivation a note that you have acquired at a discount. In the marketplace today, you will find people willing to sell notes secured by real estate. Many of these notes are bearing an eight percent, nine percent, ten percent interest rate with many years to run. These people need to sell these notes at substantial discounts in order to attract buyers. I've seen some of these long-term, low-yield notes sell for as much as a fifty percent discount.

Find Mr. Motivation and trade him a note you bought at a discount as the down payment. Trade the note at full face value.

Recently, I acquired a $61,000 third deed of trust. It had no payments on it for one year, and then it was to pay ten percent interest only. There would be a balloon payment for the principal balance, all due in five years. I offered the note at its full face value to a builder for a brand-new home in an outstanding location. The offer was accepted.

I received a legitimate $60,000 equity for my note because the builder had a problem. His construction loan time period had expired and Mr. Banker was making life rough for my builder friend. The local loan brokers would not have paid more than $35,000 cash for that note. Remember, the true Mr. Motivation isn't as motivated by profit as he is interested in getting his problem solved.

You might ask, "How do I get the money to buy the note?" Use any of the cash generating methods we have discussed so far: bank lines of credit, credit cards, friends, etc.

How do I pay short-term notes back?

1. Refinance property

2. New second mortgage on property

3. Create a new second and sell it in the marketplace

4. Roll over loan to new bank credit line, credit cards, friends, etc.

5. Find a partner

There is no limit to the innovations a lively mind can create in this real estate game. Can you come up with some solutions of your own?

Formula #34 Deep Discounted Bonds

Buy a low-yield or deep discounted bond. Some old utility bonds are only paying four percent interest rate on the face value. For these bonds to sell, the market demands that they be subject to large discounts, perhaps fifty percent or more.

You can generally buy these bonds on margin. That is, you might have to put up fifty percent of the cash, and you can borrow the remainder. Trade the bond into a free-and-clear house. You could then refinance the house. You could use these refinanced proceeds to pay off any short-term debt used to acquire the bonds. (This assumes interest rates subside.)

Why would anybody go for this? People just might feel more secure with an old A.T.&T. bond rather than holding a mortgage on a house, particularly if they are uncertain on the direction of real estate values.

Formula #35 Trade Toys

Trade any toys you have acquired during your consumer mentality days. An empire builder uses all his assets to further his progress toward wealth. A toy might be an antique or exotic car, a boat, snowmobile, motorcycle, or airplane. Use these toys as down payments on well-chosen real estate.

I know a guy who, the other day, traded his '59 Mercedes as the full down payment on a nice rental house. How did he get the Mercedes? With gemstones. How did he get the gemstones? With some currency land, for which he paid less than $25.

Do you begin to see how quickly your wealth can pyramid with the dynamic application of creative knowledge?

Barter is nothing more than finding out what the seller needs or wants and giving it to him. Try substituting barter ideas for cash today.

CHAPTER 9
Cooperative Financing:
Your Key to Success

The successful real estate empire builder knows how important it is to get the seller to carry back a substantial portion of the financing on any of his purchases. Seller financing offers more flexibility than bank financing. It can help you avoid high loan-origination fees, high interest rates, rigid qualifying requirements, and the uncertainties of adjustable rate mortgages.

Mr. Seller needs to be informed of all the various advantages to him for carrying back some or all of the financing. Convince Mr. Seller that it is in his best interest to finance the sale of his property.

SELLER BENEFITS OF COOPERATIVE FINANCING

1. Possible tax saving through an installment sale or possible combination of trade and seller financing.

2. The seller's property will sell more quickly with more flexible financing.

3. The seller might have specific money needs in the future that could be structured in a no-pay note, i.e., retirement or college.

4. Seller could be assured of a specific yield on his equity that exceeds many current savings plans.

5. His loan is secured by a piece of property he knows well.

6. He is turning an equity interest into a possible higher cash flow.

BUYER BENEFITS OF COOPERATIVE FINANCING

1. Generally, a lower interest rate.

2. Longer period of constant payments.

3. Opportunity to insert clauses beneficial to the buyer, i.e., subordination, prepay discount (see chapter on engineering paper).

4. Generally no credit check or income restrictions.

5. More flexible repayment plans.

6. Negotiable financing.

The key to the real estate empire builder's access in the next five years will be to maximize the use of seller financing. Let's look at some more no down payment formulas that involve the seller's cooperation.

Formula #36 One Hundred Percent Deal

Not long ago, I was attending an exchange meeting. A lady real estate agent announced that she had a builder client who desperately wanted out of a brand-new duplex he had just built.

I immediately cornered the agent. I discovered that the builder was interested in getting involved in a bigger and better building project. His banker wouldn't give him any more money until he sold the duplex. Also, the duplex was vacant; however, the agent assured me that she could have the units rented before a serious buyer closed escrow.

I checked with some local real estate brokers and discovered that the $51,000 sales price was very reasonable.

I made the following offer:

- Price: $51,000.

- I would assume the fixed eleven percent FHA loan of $38,000.

- I would give the seller a $13,000 second T.D. with no payments for one year. Then I would pay ten percent interest only payments monthly. The principal balance was all due in five years.

- I would put up no down payment.

- I asked that the units be rented prior to the close of escrow.

- I used the rent deposits and proration credits to cover closing costs.

The offer was accepted. I was the proud owner of a rapidly appreciating new duplex with a break-even cash flow for the first year. I was eligible for double the normal rate of depreciation because it was a new rental structure. This gave me an excellent tax shelter. All these investment benefits were obtained simply because I asked for them. The builder was off the hook with his banker; I got a super no down payment deal.

Formula #37 *Wedge and Cap*

Have Mr. Seller take out a second mortgage for the cash he needs, then have him carry back the balance of his equity in a very flexible note. This note could be secured by a third trust deed, or it might be just a personal note.

It might work like this: You meet Mr. and Mrs. Overextended. They have some pressing debts that are causing sleepless nights. They need cash to solve some of their debt problems.

Mr. and Mrs. Overextended owe $30,000 on a first T.D. This is an FHA eight percent loan with twenty-three years remaining. They are asking $60,000. This is quite a bit below the market value. But these people are desperate. They want a quick sale. They need $15,000 cash to clear up their debts.

You present the following offer:

- Price: $60,000.

- Down payment: $15,000. The sellers will obtain the $15,000 cash by putting a new second mortgage on the house.

- The sellers carry back a $15,000 note secured by a third T.D. at twelve percent interest with no payments. The principal balance is all due in five years.

- Closing costs to be paid by the seller and added on to the balance of the carryback loan.

Mr. and Mrs. Overextended are happy. They get out from under those pressing debts. Their problem is solved. You get a house for no down payment with a minimal negative cash flow because the sellers took back part of the equity with a single-payment note.

A variation to this formula might be to have the sellers create a second mortgage on their property. They could then sell this second mortgage for cash at a discount in the open market. I like using this method best because you can design the terms of the note more flexibly. You give up a larger piece of equity by the discount, but it might mean the difference between putting a high-interest-rate loan on your property or a lower-interest-rate loan with lower payments. Lower payments are critical to the real estate empire builder's ability to hold his property long enough for it to appreciate.

Formula #38   The Shotgun

Offer an all cash sale twenty-five percent below market. One way of getting this kind of offer accepted is to use the shotgun offering method discussed earlier. Literally make hundreds of offers and you will find a few getting accepted.

In the example of Mr. and Mrs. Overextended, you might offer them $25,000 cash and assume their old loan. Another way of finding these deals is to run an ad under the Real Estate Wanted column in your local newspaper. Something like this:

> I will pay all cash
> for your house in 24 hours.
> Call Ed 989-1683

A deal twenty-five percent under market is unusual, so you will have to move quickly. This is a technique in which it is vital that you have quick access to short-term funds.

How would you repay the loan? Most lenders will easily give you a loan of seventy-five percent of the market value of a house. Refinance the property and pay off your short-term debt, another one hundred percent idea for the ambitious real estate empire builder.

Formula #39   Use Mr. Seller's Credit and Time

A variation on the previous formula might work like this: Have the seller put a new first mortgage on his property. You would then give Mr. Seller a note for the balance of his equity.

It is best to have the seller put on the financing for several reasons:

- Applying for a loan is time-consuming. Your time is a valuable asset.

- You won't have to qualify for the loan if you buy the property subject to the loan. You are supplying the ideas.

- Mr. Seller is supplying the legwork and credit. Both of you win.

This is a common formula for investors to use today. Let's assume that the seller insists that you get the new loan. You might use any of the following formulas.

Formula #40   The Flexible Barter System

Exchange some item that has a flexible value, such as artwork, gemstones, currency land, antiques, etc. Use one or more of these items as a down payment. The lending institution may accept these items, instead of a cash down payment, as valuable considerations. FHA, for instance, will allow you to use notes and other items with an established value as down payments on properties.

Let us say that Mr. Motivation is willing to sell you his house for $60,000. You figure the house might be worth $50,000 tops! You say, "Mr. Motivation, I will pay you $60,000 for your house." Mr. Motivation almost falls out of his chair lurching for the pen to sign the agreement. He never thought he would get that outrageous price.

"Not so fast, Mr. Motivation," you say. "I will give you $48,000 cash and two $6,000 recreational lots I own." The highest and best use for these lots is having them hold the earth together. (You can pick up lots like these in many areas of the country for back taxes, in some cases as cheaply as $25 apiece.)

The seller's "greed grin" fades. You explain that in essence, you are offering $48,000 cash that the bank will loan on the property, with the remainder of the inflated equity to be exchanged for recreational lots. You might add that the equity above $48,000 is as questionable as the recreational lot value.

Formula #41   The Work Credit

Structure a transaction where the seller transfers back part of the cash in the deal after the close of escrow. The most common way this is done is by the seller giving the buyer a work credit.

It works something like this: You and the seller agree to a price. Your price might be established based on the house being in good repair. Let us say that the price is $75,000. The house does have some deferred maintenance such as flaky paint, stained carpets, and a rotten bathroom floor (very common). You and the seller agree that the cost to repair the house could run up to $25,000. It is up to the buyer and seller to agree to this. The bank will loan you $60,000, or approximately eighty percent of the purchase price. The seller agrees to give you a work credit for $15,000 to do the repairs.

$$\begin{array}{r} \$15,000 \text{ Work credit} \\ +\ \underline{60,000 \text{ Bank loan}} \\ \$75,000 \text{ Purchase price} \end{array}$$

Your title company can handle the mechanics of the paperwork.

The net result of this deal is that you get into the property for no down payment. However, in essence you just deferred the down payment, as the repairs will need to be done; but perhaps, being a creative real estate empire builder, you can figure out a way to defer that cost also, perhaps by bartering for services and materials.

Some lending institutions might insist on impounding the funds and disbursing the cash as work is done.

Formula #42   Blanket Mortgage

If Mr. Seller balks at carrying back one hundred percent financing, offer him more security. Make him warm and cozy with a blanket mortgage.

A blanket mortgage basically gives Mr. Seller a mort-

gage on more than one property. You find that Mr. Seller
is possibly willing to take all paper for his equity. However, he is still a bit hesitant. He would like more security,
so that he knows you won't just walk away from the
property.

Let us say that you want to acquire a nice little rental
house for $65,000. The seller will carry one hundred per-
cent of the financing if you will provide some additional
security. You offer the seller a blanket mortgage on a
house you own (or you are able to borrow from friend or
family) that has approximately $30,000 equity in it, and on
the seller's house also.

He should feel very secure with this setup. This is a
good technique when you are short on cash and long on
equities. Try to have an escape provision for your blanket,
such as once the appraised value of the seller's house
reaches a certain point, the additional security is released
from the blanket encumbrance.

If you don't have a release provision, you begin to build
inflexibility into your real estate portfolio; i.e., you can't
refinance properties separately and can't sell them separately. An empire builder always structures flexibility into
his deals at the outset of a transaction.

Formula #43   *Discounted Price Plus Refinancing*

Offer a seller all cash if the seller agrees to discount the
price. In today's market, this can be accomplished quite
easily. Now comes the real magic to this formula. Negotiate to buy out the holder of the notes on the property at a
discount. This gives you two ways of discounting the
price to, say, seventy-five percent or eighty percent of the
current market value.

You could then go out and get a lending institution to
lend you enough cash to finance the deal one hundred
percent. Of course, you will need to structure this carefully. Generally, Mr. Lender does not like to give you one
hundred percent financing, so you may have to use your
line of credit at the bank to close the deal initially. Then
you could go back and refinance the house to generate the
cash required to pay off the short-term loan.

For example, let's assume that Mr. Seller is asking $75,000 for his house; he owes $40,000. That makes his equity $35,000. Mr. Seller agrees to accept $20,000 for his equity for a quick sale. He desperately needs the money! You agree to pay the $20,000 cash for Mr. Seller's equity subject to the private note holder agreeing to discount his note to $30,000 for cash. Mr. Seller agrees. You approach Mr. Note Holder and offer him $30,000 for his $40,000 note. He accepts your offer, since his note has many more years to run. Mr. Note Holder sees the fixed payments he gets from the note decreasing in purchasing power because of inflation. He is willing to take a discount in order to have his cash back now to reinvest at today's higher yields.

Through some creative effort, we have succeeded in lowering the price of the house from $75,000 to $50,000. Mr. Lender should easily lend us the $50,000 we need to close the deal. That is a good safe loan. If he won't lend us the money, close it with other short-term lines of credit and side agreements, and then refinance to pay off short-term debts. Fourteen or fifteen of these types of deals will give you a million dollars in property—a quick and specific way to a future million-dollar net worth. Warning: Refinancing above fourteen percent interest rates will jeopardize any equity you thought you had as a result of buying at such a low price.

With a little digging, you will find an abundance of opportunities to build your real estate empire.

Formula #44 Pay a Higher Price

In most cases, you can pay a higher price on a property if the terms are sufficiently flexible. Let us look at an example:

Which deal would you choose? Assume that each of these proposed financing packages apply to the same property.

A. Asking price $60,000
    Down payment   6,000
                  $54,000   1st T.D. owner carryback 12% interest only with a balloon payment due in 3 years; monthly payment to be $540.

B.	Price	$75,000	1st T.D. owner carryback
	Down payment	-0-	at 8% interest with the
			balance due in 10 years.
			Payments: $500.00.

That was a loaded question! You would probably be better off in the second example. Why?

- Lower interest rate
- Lower payments
- Longer due date

You can afford to sacrifice price for flexible terms. These above three items must never automatically be given up by the empire builder during negotiations. The terms of a transaction are just as important as the price, and in some cases more important, particularly if it means the difference between you holding on to a property or losing it because of difficult terms. It doesn't matter what kind of price break you get on a piece of property, if you can't hold on to its future rewards, your efforts will have been fruitless.

As a real estate empire builder, you should have a good financial calculator available. I use a Hewlett-Packard 38E. It is an indispensable tool for making trade-off decisions between price and terms.

Formula #45 *Contract of Sale*

Mr. Seller might be willing to sell you his property on a contract of sale. It is also known as a land sales contract or agreement of sale. Basically, title is still vested with the owner (seller). You obtain an equitable interest in the property. The contract of sale should be recorded to assure that your claim on the property is in the public record.

Many sellers are willing to sell for no down payment if they can retain title. The contract should stipulate, however, that as soon as certain predetermined conditions are satisfied, the title should be transferred to the buyer. "Certain conditions" might include a future cash down payment, or when the property is rehabilitated, or when the appraised value is a specific price.

In California, it might take a year for a seller to get his property back in case of a default when using a contract of sale. This is in contrast to about four months if the property is sold and the seller carries back a note secured by a trust deed. For this reason, it may not be good to sell on a contract; but to buy with a contract of sale might further limit your risk and thus be to the buyer's advantage because of the longer foreclosure period.

When attempting to get the seller to cooperate on the financing, it is very important to make him feel secure. It also is vital that you structure the proper financial incentives, i.e., tax, interest, and payback period. Insist that the seller participate in the financing. This is crucial to your making money in real estate. Use the tools you have gathered to meet the seller's concerns, and your fortune will be well in hand.

CHAPTER 10
Options: The Ultimate Investment Tool

A wise man once said, "Property has its duties as well as its rights." All of you who now own property know exactly what I mean—monthly payments, negative cash flow, sewer plug-ups, rent collection, tax and insurance bills, tenant squabbles. These are some of the prices we pay for property ownership.

Why do property owners put up with these aggravations? Very simply, it is worth the price. Any investment that can consistently bring you twenty-five percent, fifty percent, one hundred percent, two hundred percent returns on your money must always have a little bit of anguish associated with it.

Not so fast! What if I could show you a real estate investment tool that harnesses the exceptional real estate benefit of appreciation without the associated costs? The well-designed option is such a tool.

THE ULTIMATE INVESTMENT TOOL

The legal definition of an option is, "a contract to keep an offer open." Basically, in real estate it is applied in this manner: It gives one person (optionee) the right to buy, sell, lease, exchange, or mortgage a piece of property from another person (optionor). The parties included must conform to specific terms and conditions within a set time period.

Formula #46   The Pure Option

Let's say that you meet Mr. Farmer, who lives on the edge of town. Through discussion, you find that Mr. Farmer is concerned that his land value might be falling because of poor-yielding soil. You think that Mr. Farmer's land is in the path of urban growth, but you will have to wait at least three years to be sure.

Mr. Farmer feels his land is worth $1,000,000. You offer Mr. Farmer $5,000 for an option to buy his land at any time within the next thee years for $1,000,000 on mutually acceptable terms. Mr. Farmer accepts, and Mr. Farmer gets money now to do with as he wants. He gets some minor protection from a decline in market values.

What do you get? With a relatively small "chunk" of cash you control the phenomenal appreciation potential of this $1,000,000 piece of ground. If you guessed correctly, this ground could be worth $2,000,000 in three years. This is an example of how, with one small deal, you could catapult yourself into a real estate empire.

The great news is that you have no tenants, you pay no taxes or insurance, and you have no monthly "alligators" nipping at your financial heels. With the option, you have locked in the potential appreciation with none of the detrimental costs of ownership. Of course, if values do go down and you don't exercise your option, you would lose the option money. However, if you have adequately done your homework, you can minimize the chances of total loss.

The option is a vital tool for the empire builder. Let us examine some more options and formulas that can leverage you to riches.

Formula #47   Debt Relief Option

Mr. and Mrs. Motivation have debt problems. They are getting the squeeze from their local collection agency. Their debts only total $1,000; but for these people under pressure, with no means of getting it paid, it might as well be a million.

Mr. and Mrs. Motivation have determined that the only way to solve their problem and take care of their debt is to sell the house. They are asking $60,000. You sit down with them and ask, "Where will you go if the house sells?"

They say that they are not sure: "Rent or something else, I guess," they answer.

"You still owe $50,000 on the house, right?" you ask.

They nod yes.

"Instead of selling your house, why don't you give me an option to buy it at its current price for three years? I will even pay you all cash for today's equity in three years. In exchange for the option, Mr. and Mrs. Motivation, I will assume your $1,000 debt today. You won't have to move from your house; you will get all cash for your equity when I exercise the option, and you get out from under those pressuring debts."

If Mr. and Mrs. Motivation accept, contact the collection agency and try to work out an easy repayment schedule of the debts on behalf of Mr. and Mrs. Motivation. Borrow the money short-term and buy out the debts at a discount. Creatively work to lower your effective option consideration.

If Mr. and Mrs. Motivation balk at your offer, attempt to option fifty percent of the house. What you are doing is locking in the appreciating ability of the single family house for little or no cash. I recently solved a debt problem of this sort and received an option on one third of a house. If you are betting that well-selected houses are going to appreciate over the next few years, as I do, find a Mr. and Mrs. Motivation and option all or even a part of their house.

Let's look at your potential profit in the latest instance. In three years, given a ten percent appreciation rate, that house might be worth $81,000. ($81,000–$60,000 = $21,000 gross profit.) If you subtract your maximum investment of $1,000 cash, your net gain before taxes would be approximately $20,000—and you did not have the problems of property ownership. It will not take too many of these to put your empire in the millions quickly. Start now!

Formula #48   Note as Option

Use a promissory note instead of cash for option consideration. You might also use postdated checks, bank drafts, money market fund checks, or any legitimate means by which you can harness the appreciation benefits of real estate today and pay tomorrow with dollars cheapened by inflation.

This note could be secured or unsecured. If it needs to be secured, try securing it with a piece of real estate you own or a piece you can borrow. Attempt to make any cash payment due at the time you exercise the option—as far into the future as possible.

You might also attempt to secure a note with a friend's certificate of deposit, trust deed, T-bills, government bonds, stocks, etc.

Formula #49   Dream as Option

Dreams make good vehicles for options. Mr. and Mrs. Consumer would love to go to Hawaii. They just never had the spare cash to get there. Give Mr. and Mrs. Consumer the trip to Hawaii in exchange for an option to purchase all or part of their home.

You might be able to arrange a trade for a week in a condominium in Hawaii. Contact media brokers who sometimes have airline tickets for trade. Substitute talent and ideas for cash whenever possible, i.e., use credit cards, installment loans, trades, etc.

Mr. and Mrs. Consumer run on emotional, nonprofit-oriented modes. You, as a real estate empire builder, must recognize this fact and fill their needs accordingly. Give Mr. and Mrs. Consumer their toys and dreams today. You will be rich tomorrow by effectively using these as an option device.

Formula #50   Equity as Option

Use equity in an existing property as option consideration. It's best to use currency items for this, unless you are absolutely secure about the future price movements of a property, e.g., you've got some inside information on a zoning change. As mentioned before, currency property might include recreational lots, gemstones, scrip for services, etc.

By harnessing the appreciating benefits of a nice piece of property and by using unsaleable property as option consideration, we begin to unlock hidden assets in our real estate portfolio. All property has value. It depends on the ideas applied to that property to ultimately determine its real value. By placing a piece of currency ground into a problem, you have just taken a step toward increasing your real net worth.

Formula #51   Sweat as Option

Offer the use of your abilities, skills, or just labor as consideration for an option. I have a budding real estate empire builder friend who has acquired an option to buy fifty percent in several houses. He finds run-down properties badly in need of repairs. He contacts the owner and offers his labor and carpentry skills as consideration for an option. His proposition goes something like this: "You buy the materials and I'll fix up the house and manage it. In exchange, I want an option to buy fifty percent of your house for one dollar at any time during the next five years."

That's a good deal for both parties. An out-of-town owner with a vacant house needs an empire builder to restore and save his real estate investment.

Drive around various neighborhoods. When you spot a run-down house, take note of the address. Ask neighbors who owns the house. They will generally know. If they don't know, you can find out from the county tax records. These owners need help! You can help them and yourself with a sweat option.

Formula #52   The Rolling Option

The rolling option basically allows you to control a small portion or tract of a larger piece of property. (This is a tool usually used in land developments, but also may be used with housing tracts or condominium developments.) If you meet with success with the smaller portion through rezoning, a favorable resale, etc., your original option would then roll over to another portion or all of the remaining condos or housing units.

For example, you have just found a promising thirty-acre parcel in the path of growth outside your town. The owner wants $15,000 per acre for it. Because of uncertain economic conditions, you are not sure that you want to risk buying the entire property.

You decide to option five of the thirty acres. The option consideration is $1,000. That is the kind of superleverage that yields big potential profits. The land is already split into five-acre parcels. If you meet with success in marketing the first five-acre parcel, you can then exercise the option and buy the land, or just transfer the option to a new optionee. Built into the rollover option agreement is a statement that simply says, "If optionee exercises option on parcel #1 he then has an option to buy parcel #2," and so on. Be sure to consult a competent real estate attorney before you draft this type of option.

Formula #53   Creative Variation

A variation on the rolling option idea might work like this: Go to the courthouse and, with some research, find an old subdivision. Everything has been plotted and divided, but for some reason the lots have never been sold. The original owner still owns the lots.

My friend Rick ran into such a deal. He called the owner and asked, "How would you like to convert the dead equity in that old subdivision into a secure income?"

The owner liked the idea. With some research, Rick found that the land in this area was selling for about $700 per acre. However, he also discovered that lots near this area were selling for about $3,000 apiece. Rick smelled a profit.

He made the following offer to Mr. Dead Equity:

- For one dollar and other valuable consideration, I option lots 1–10 for ninety days. The exercise price will be $700 a lot.

- If I exercise my option, the terms of the sale will be as follows: Payments to be made in sixty equal monthly installments including ten percent interest.

- Also, I have the right to substitute collateral to property of equal or greater value. (This means that the buyer can take the loan off this property, making it free and clear. The buyer can then secure the loan with another property. This is called definancing a property.)

- If I exercise this option, I have the right to option lots 11–20, and so on . . .

The offer was accepted by Mr. Dead Equity.

Rick then went out and found Mr. Motivation. Mr. Motivation owned an apartment building that had some management problems. He wanted out! Rick, being a creative empire builder, surveyed the situation and decided that he could solve the building's management problems.

Rick offered Mr. Motivation the first ten lots of the optioned subdivision. The exchange value would be $3,000 per lot, or $30,000 as a down payment on the apartment building.

How was Rick able to deliver the lots free and clear to Mr. Motivation? There was sufficient equity in the apartment building for Rick to move the loans from the lots to the newly acquired apartment building. He substituted the apartment building as collateral. The owner of the lots was happy. He converted a dead equity into an income stream secured by improved property. Mr. Motivation was happy, as he exchanged a management-problem piece of real estate for a management-free property.

Rick optioned the remainder of the lots in the subdivision and proceeded to trade them into other improved properties. Starting with the simple option idea, Rick was able to pyramid himself to $75,000 in solid equities within six months starting with only one dollar. Rick truly deserves the empire builder's "Creating Something from Nothing" award.

Formula #54   *Option for an Option*

Try an option for an option as consideration. As you become more experienced in the option game, you can further leverage the options that you own.

Give Mr. Motivation an option to buy a nice apartment building; in exchange, you might get an option to buy his house. Why would Mr. Motivation do this? He might think that your well-located apartment building will rise in value faster than his house. He is accepting your option as a hedge against a possible decline in the value of his home.

Formula #55   *Exchangeable Equity Option*

If you have locked in a low enough price, for a long enough time period, and with favorable terms, the chances are pretty good that your option was valued in excess of the consideration paid. You can use that value or equity in an option in place of a cash down payment on a house.

For example, let's say that I option an apartment building for $1,000 for one year. The building has a fifteen percent vacancy factor. I am willing to pay the current market value of $300,000 for this building.

I am interested in this project because I have discovered that a large manufacturing company is moving into the area soon. The company plans to bring more employees, which should eliminate my vacancy problem. This reduction of vacancies should increase the value of the building to (let's say) $350,000. I now have a $50,000 exchangeable equity in my option.

I find Mr. Up and Coming Seller. He sees an opportunity to trade his house for an option on a nice apartment building in a growing area. Mr. Up and Coming Seller might see it as a way to get out of troublesome rental house into hassle-free appreciation.

Options don't just apply to real estate, they have been used in the stock market for many years. What are some of the other items in which you could create an exchangeable equity using options?

- Leases

- Cars, boats to buy

- Notes, mortgages, trust deeds

- Vacation time

- Income flows through trusts

You can option almost anything on which there is a delayed acceptance situation. Use your imagination. What do you have of value? What *will* you have of value? Use these hidden assets as options to control well-selected real estate. The ideal exchange of options for real estate occurs when you trade your depreciating assets for appreciating real property, i.e., personal property, boats, or cars for real properties such as houses, condominiums, etc.

THE KEYS FOR MAKING THE OPTION WORK

1. Lock in the exercise price on the option in terms of today's value so that you can control the benefits of future appreciation.

2. Always have your options notarized and recorded in the county courthouse.

3. Before recording an option, always get a preliminary title report so that you can verify information given you by the optionor.

4. An option that you own is saleable or exchangeable; if you have structured it properly, there should be a real exchangeable value in that option.

5. The key to making money with an option is leverage. Put the smallest amount of consideration down to control the largest amount of property.

6. Get the longest time period possible.

7. Adequately address possible future problems in your option agreement. E.g.:

   • Optionor takes out another loan
   • Bankruptcy
   • Insurance coverage
   • Eminent domain
   • What happens in case of death of owner
   • Default on loans
   • Care of property

Use a good real estate attorney to draft an option that conforms with your local and state laws. Use the option to control a hassle-free real estate empire.

CHAPTER 11
Lease-Options

The lease with an option to purchase, or lease-option as it's commonly called, allows you to control the appreciation benefits of a property; it also grants you use of the property itself. This investment tool, if properly used, can be an invaluable asset in the empire builder's repertoire of no down payment formulas.

The main purpose of entering into a lease-option agreement is to control the future appreciation benefits of the property; however, unlike the case with a pure option, you would probably be involved with management if you chose to rent out the building rather than live in it yourself.

It is not the totally ideal "hassle-free" investment of a straight or pure option; however, let's look at how being involved with management can increase your success ratio in getting options accepted.

The lease option can be a very flexible real estate investment tool. *There is no such thing as a standard agreement.* All provisions, clauses, costs, credits, terms at sale, option consideration, and time frames are negotiable. Therefore, negotiations for a lease-option should be considered to have the same importance as if it were a sale. It is, after all, a delayed sale with the right to use the property for the lease period.

Let's look at how the lease-option can provide benefits for the lessor, lessee, buyer, and seller.

LEASE-OPTIONS UNLOCK HIDDEN PROFITS

The lease-option is probably the easiest way of gaining control of property without cash that I know—if you know what you are doing.

People ask, "Where do I find owners who will lease-option their property?" On any particular day, you can look through the real estate classified section of your newspaper and see several ads advertising lease-options. The ad headline might read:

- Possible lease with an option to purchase
- Owner bought another house
- Owner transferred
- Owner desperate
- House vacant

Any ad in which the owner is suggesting a lease-option or that he is handling a financially crippling payment indicates to the real estate empire builder that there is an opportunity to solve a problem—and make a profit. The lease-option can offer a viable solution to unlocking those profits.

Formula #56   Homes for Rent Technique

Another method used to prospect for lease-options is to look in the "Homes for Rent or Lease" section of the newspaper. Try to spot ads of landlords who have possible monthly payment problems. They might be out-of-town owners who do not have the time or interest to take care of the property.

In many instances, the real estate empire builder needs to find owners who are not motivated purely by profit to turn this idea into a gold mine. For instance, you call on a "House for Rent" ad that has an out-of-town phone number; you find out that the house has been vacant for some time. *This fact alone has to create anxiety in even the wealthiest owners.* A vacant house is vulnerable to vandalism, and it produces no rent with which to make payments, all of which creates innumerable gray hairs on Mr. Motivation's already "patchy" scalp.

Mr. Motivation has a problem! Have you ever tried to rent a house when you live one hundred miles away and don't have the assistance of professional management? I have . . . and it isn't easy!

Mr. Motivation needs you! Propose to Mr. Motivation that you would be willing to lease the house for a five-year period. Mr. Motivation might begin to drool in his excitement as he thinks, "That would mean no more management for five years . . . no vacancies, no tenant hassles . . . I could still get the tax shelter."

You also mention to Mr. Motivation that you will take care of all maintenance up to $25 per month, if he agrees to lower the lease payment a bit and keep the payment the same for five years. Let's say you request a rent reduction of $25 per month.

Remember to remain flexible. If Mr. Motivation balks at any of your terms, ask him, "What would you suggest?"

Get the owners moving in a positive direction to create a successful deal.

Mr. and Mrs. Motivation need your suggestions. Mr. and Mrs. Motivation can be heard over the phone in the background jumping up and down and singing, "Hallelujah." You are helping them solve their property problem; now it is their turn to help you solve your problem of building a real estate empire.

You interrupt their joy by saying, "Yeah, I'd be willing to give you a management-free, maintenance-free investment for five years. You can check out my references. You'll find that I am a responsible, ambitious guy. I only want one additional item in return."

"What's that?" Mr. and Mrs. Motivation giggle.

"I want an option to purchase the house at any time within the next five years at its appraised value today."

Mr. and Mrs. Motivation gasp, "What?"

You calm them down and go over the benefits they will derive from such a transaction:

- They get five years' tax benefits.

- They have a management- and trouble-free investment.

- You will pay them all cash for their "dog" of a house at the time you exercise the option.

If you get further objections, be flexible! Be creative! Let's look at some variations to this theme.

Formula #57   Lease-Option Variations

A variation to the above formula might include any of the following compromises:

1. In exchange for the lease-option, you could share the appreciation with the owners. I wouldn't put up with the responsibility of management unless I received control of at least fifty percent of the appreciation benefits.

2. You might give Mr. and Mrs. Motivation a specific after-tax return on their equity. For example, I have a friend who recently lease-optioned a property. His

> exercise price was subordinate to the owner getting a
> sixteen percent after-tax return on his "current equity."

Also, it might be a good idea to only use this second variation when the owner has a small equity. Otherwise, you might be guaranteeing an appreciation rate that exceeds the appreciation rate you were expecting to obtain. You are betting on the continued upward movement of real estate prices. I think that is a good bet!

Formula #58 *Credits: Just Like a Low-Interest Loan*

When negotiating for a lease-option, work hard to get maximum credit for your lease payment applied toward the purchase price.

For example, if you negotiate a lease payment of $500 per month, try to get $50 or $100 or more of that amount applied toward a dollar-for-dollar reduction in the purchase price. If you receive a $100-a-month credit and your lease-option period is for two years, you would receive (24 months x $100 =) $2,400 as a direct reduction in the purchase price. Probably, in keeping with the no down payment philosophy, you would want to use that credit to reduce any future cash down payment.

Generally, the most outstanding feature of a lease-option is that it allows you to control a property's appreciation at only the amount it would cost to rent and only a fraction of the amount it would cost you to buy.

Formula #59 *No Down Payment, No Interest*

Convince Mr. Motivation to let you lease-option his house in exchange for some ability you might have, i.e., cleaning the house, painting, management, etc. You will have just acquired control of the appreciation in a piece of real estate. Great! The true empire builder doesn't stop here! He always finds ways to turn a good deal into a super deal! Here is one way! Convince the lessor to apply one hundred percent of the lease payment to a direct reduction in price. Remember, you'll be paying that price at some future date.

In our previous example, we talked about payments of

REAL ESTATE PURCHASE AGREEMENT
AND RECEIPT FOR DEPOSIT

This is intended to be a legally binding contract. Read it carefully.

_____ , _____ , 19 _____
(City)   (State)

Received from _____ ,
(Name)

herein called Buyer, the sum of _____
sixty thousand _____ dollars $ 60,000 _____ , in the form of cash □,

cashier's check □ personal check □ or _____ □ payable to
(Name) _____ , to be held uncashed

until acceptance of this offer, as deposit on account of purchase price of _____
_____ dollars $ _____

for the purchase of property located in _____ ,
(City)

County of _____ , _____ ,
(County)   (State)

described as follows: _____
(Address or other legal description)

Buyer will deposit in escrow with _____
(Title company or other third party)

the balance of purchase price as follows: _____

   1.   This is a 2-year lease-option agreement.

   2.   Buyer to pay monthly rental payments of $500 per month.

   3.   When option is exercised, buyer will receive $100 per
      month credit toward purchase.

   4.   Sales price at time of exercise of option is $60,000.

   5.   Buyer will assume existing loan of approximately $43,000.
      Seller will carry back remainder of sales price less credit
      in note and deed of trust at 10% interest with all principal
      and interest due in 5 years from closing.

   6.   Buyer to maintain property in present condition.

   7.   Buyer has the right to sublet property.

   8.   If buyer fails to exercise option within the option period,
      all payments will be considered rent.

Detail above any factual terms and conditions applicable to this sale, such as financing, contingency of sale of other property, the disposition of structural pest control inspection, and repairs and personal property to be included in the sale.

Deposit will □ will not □ be increased by $ _____ to $ _____
within _____ days of acceptance of this offer.

Buyer does □ does not □ intend to occupy subject property as his residence.

The supplements initialed below are incorporated as part of this agreement.

_____ Structural Pest Control Certification Agreement   _____ VA Amendment

_____ Special Studies Zone Disclosure   _____ FHA Amendment

_____ Flood Insurance Disclosure   _____ Other _____

_____ Occupancy Agreement   _____ Other _____

Buyer and Seller acknowledge receipt of a copy of this page, which constitutes page 1 of _____ Pages.

X _____   X _____
  Buyer   Seller

X _____   X _____
  Buyer   Seller

$500 per month for two years. If we assume that the price of the house is $75,000, at the time we exercise our option in two years, the amount of the total payments paid would be (24 x $500 =)$12,000, so the purchase price is $75,000 less $12,000 = $63,000 as the new purchase price, or the amount we owe at the end of two years. How quickly could you save money for a down payment if you had no monthly housing expense? Your entire monthly payment could be applied directly toward that future cash down payment. In this case, if the required future cash down payment was to be $12,000 you would have no down payment left to pay at the end of the two years.

When approaching sellers on this type of lease-option, rather than explaining the $12,000 reduction as reducing the cost, talk about it in terms of a *deferred down payment*.

If you meet with resistance, be flexible! Try any of the following variations; but most of all, try something today!

- Raise the price and increase the credit in a proportion that will still benefit you and the seller.

- Have the credit vary seasonally. Suggest Christmas as a good time to give a one hundred percent credit.

- Exchange other services for an increase in the credit, a labor for lease payment trade-off.

Formula #60 No Down Payment, No Interest and No Payments

Does that sound incredible? Unbelievable? It shouldn't for the budding empire builder. If you haven't got the point by now, *ideas create wealth* . . . and the ideas available are infinite. Get determined and tap into that source of infinite wealth.

This wealth-building idea has worked for many others and will work for you. Find a Mr. Motivation, a guy who is having chronic management problems with apartments that he owns; there should be at least four units in the building or on the property.

Offer Mr. Motivation an end to his management head-aches. Ask him if he would be willing to lease the apartment building to you for a five-year period. Indicate also that you would like an option to buy it any time during that five-year lease period. You might further request that he lease it to you below what the scheduled rents would be. You might point out that, because of the rent collection problems and vacancies, he is probably not getting all of his rents anyway. "With me, you could be certain to get the rents," you add.

You might consider furnishing references to make him feel secure, safe, and cozy at night. References don't necessarily need to be financial in nature; they can be just character references. Remember, he really wants you to solve his problem. Most people pay dearly to have problems solved.

You examine the rent schedule and, based on the local rental market, you decide that rents are low anyway. With a little "grit and muscle" and creativity, you feel that you can solve the management problems.

Mr. Motivation sees relief for the chief aggravation in his life and goes for the deal. You move into one of the apartments. You take control of the management situation, evict the "deadbeats," fill the vacancies, and generally improve the living conditions and raise the rents.

By raising the rents, you can have the tenants actually pay your rent plus a profitable cash flow, if the deal is structured properly. This particular lease-option might be structured so that one hundred percent of the lessee payment is applied toward the direct reduction of principal. (Generally, it would be difficult to get this provision for more than one year, but it is worth trying.) This means that no interest is paid on the apartment building asset you are controlling, no payments are being made by you, and you have a free place to live. You have successfully harnessed the appreciation of the greatest moneymaking machine of our time: well-managed income property.

CHAPTER 12
Playing with Escrows and Agents

Within any given transaction, there generally are a couple of hidden cash generators. Escrows and real estate agents provide the key to many of these cash sources. They also provide various mechanisms by which we can maximize the gain on our investment with minimum capital and time inputs.

Let's examine how escrows and real estate agents can help us build our real estate empire.

Formula #61   The Agent's Commission

Use the agent's commission to reduce your cash down payment. Let's say that Mr. Real Estate Agent has brought to your attention a nice rental house. Its price is $60,000. Mr. Agent says, "The down payment is only $5,000 and the owner will carry back the balance." What is Mr. Agent really telling you? *The owner is willing to sell for no down payment!*

The agent is the person who needs the money, not the seller. His expected commission would normally be (6% x $60,000=) $3,600. That leaves approximately $1,400 ($5,000 –$3,600=$1,400) for the seller. Five hundred dollars might go for closing costs, so Mr. Seller is expecting a grand total of $900 cash out of the deal. That does not constitute a significant incentive to sell. Mr. Seller will probably do the deal without getting any cash. It appears that generating cash is not the prime motivation for selling.

The guy that wants the cash, Mr. R.E. Agent, is the person with whom you should be negotiating concerning cash down payment. Ask Mr. Agent to take his commission back as a note secured by the property. Give him periodic payments if he insists, such as monthly, quarterly, or annually. I would rather give Mr. R.E. Agent a single-payment note: no payments, with the principal balance and accrued interest all due in a year or two, or whenever the property is resold. You have deferred that cash expenditure to a future date. This is an important rule in the Conservation of Cash Philosophy. Buy an appreciating real estate asset today, and pay for it tomorrow.

If Mr. R.E. Agent needs food money, negotiate a partial payment of the commission, with him taking the remainder of his commission in the form of a note. This partial cash commission is normally done much more easily. Also, it will give Mr. R.E. Agent some incentive to continue to bring you good deals. (Also consider bartering for the commission.)

Formula #62   The Agent's Cash Sources

Mr. Real Estate Agent may be a source of additional cash needed to close a transaction. It might be his own cash! If Mr. R.E. Agent is successful, he might have some spare cash to put into a second or third mortgage on your would-be property. If he doesn't have any extra cash, he might know where to get some. A good realtor keeps tabs on friends, family, investors, etc., who have cash available and who want to put it to use in high-yield debt instruments, i.e., mortgages, trust deeds, and unsecured notes.

Formula #63   *The Eleventh-Hour Squeeze*

Let's say that you are getting right down to the wire and it appears that you won't have enough cash to close the escrow. No ulcers, please! Worrying is destructive! It only diverts the empire builder's vital creative energies from solutions. Think solutions!

Let's first ask, "Who has a vested interest in closing the escrow?"

- The real estate agent

- The seller

First, find out how Mr. Agent might be able to help you with that cash shortage problem. He's dying to close the deal. He's already spent his commission, either in reality or just psychologically. You approach him and indicate that you don't have enough cash to close the deal, and if you don't close, Mr. Agent can wave bye-bye to his commission.

Mr. Agent becomes depressed and suicidal; but you, being a positive force in the world, say, "There might be one way of saving the deal!"

"What is it?" he chokes.

"If you would be willing to lend me part of the commission back on the deal, I think that we can close."

He might retort, "I already told you that I wouldn't do that."

You point out that he is entitled to change his mind, particularly if he wants to get paid.

I don't mean to suggest that this technique should be used callously, but when a close is near, you need to use the motivations of all parties involved to complete an otherwise dead deal. The true empire builder will identify and use these motivations to solve all wealth-building problems.

Formula #64   *More Help from Mr. Seller*

As the close of escrow nears, Mr. Seller begins forming ideas about how he will spend his money. My experience has shown that the nearer a transaction gets to closing, the more definite the seller's plans become on how he will spend his cash; or how nice it will be to be free of that management headache; or other similar motivations.

Go through the same explanation with Mr. Seller as you did with Mr. Agent. This is the ideal time to renegotiate a deal, if it is done tactfully.

The following items might be renegotiated in order to lower your cash down payment prior to closing escrow.

- Seller can take a larger note

- Seller can take a personal note

- Seller can take a short-term payoff note, i.e., high payments, maybe high interest rate

- Seller can take a short-term single payment note

- Seller can exchange part of his down payment for a service, a dream, or currency items

- Seller can pay all closing costs

- Seller can allow taxes to go unpaid

- Seller can allow insurance to be placed on a monthly payment schedule

Find out what the seller has finally decided to do with the money he will receive. He might be more receptive to you buying that dream for him just prior to the close of escrow than he was during that pressurized negotiation period.

One caution: Be very careful and tactful during this time. Don't nickel and dime the deal to death. Explain to the seller exactly how much cash you are short. Try to establish a "working together to solve the problem" spirit, rather than an adversary relationship. Try to move toward mutually beneficial solutions.

Formula #65   *Profits from the Delayed Closing*

The delayed close offers many of the same advantages as an option. In this case, you can control the potential appreciation benefits without owning the property itself, just a right to buy it for some limited period!

It works very simply. Let's assume that you have agreed on the terms with Mr. Seller. He has agreed to take $5,000 down and he will carry back a $50,000 note for the remainder of his equity. You figure that it is an exceptional deal.

You have only one minor problem. You don't have $5,000! You have gathered the necessary techniques in *No Down Payment Formulas* so far to generate that much cash, or you could use a partner to put up the cash (more about that in a future chapter). However, let's assume that you plan to resell this house for a quick profit while it is still in escrow. A nice chunk of cash would sure come in handy for other projects in which you are involved—like buying groceries, paying the phone bill, etc.

Instead of working to close escrow, you want it delayed as long as possible—ninety days, one hundred twenty days, or more. The earnest money might be in the form of a postdated check or a personal note so that you don't have any money tied up in escrow. Your game plan is to sell the house prior to the close of escrow.

This formula is best used when you have come upon a super deal, well below market, or in a market with rapidly rising prices.

I have used this technique quite successfully to generate periodic sources of cash flow. Once the empire builder gains that vital knowledge of the market, he will be digging up great deals all day long. Market knowledge is a must if you want to play this game successfully.

In your purchase agreement, make sure that you have written in the proper clauses. For example: *Buyer has the right to show the property by giving the seller twenty-four hours notice at any time during the escrow period.*

This is a tricky proposition! Some sellers, if they get wind of what you are trying to do, might attempt to get in your way. You'll have to be a real juggler at times to pull this one off.

Before signing the purchase agreement, make sure that you have included the proper weasel clause or contingencies, such as *this offer is subject to my partner's inspection.*

If you are not able to resell the property before escrow closes, this weasel clause will allow you to bow out gracefully. Just write a note to Mr. Seller or his agent explaining that your partner doesn't approve of the property.

For a quick sale, and quick profit, price the property below the current market. Remember, *you need to attract immediate attention!* Also, when writing the purchase agreement, make sure that where it says "Buyer," you put your name and then add the words "or assigns." This clause might prevent any future problems once you have found a new buyer.

When selling a property, gain maximum exposure; advertise in the newspaper, hand out 8½ x 11" sheets, let the newspaper carriers distribute flyers. Let the world know about your property.

I met a guy recently who puts a large sign on the side of his panel truck. The sign says:

> $1,000 finder's fee for
> anyone who brings me
> a buyer for my house
> Price $75,000—Call 000 000-0000

He tells me that after a day of driving around, he might get as many as ten phone calls in the evening responding to this unusual ad. Innovative approaches to old problems create wealth.

Formula #66   *The Double Escrow*

The double escrow is one of the real ideal no down payment formulas. You can have your cake and eat it, too.

A few years ago I decided to make an offer on four houses that were sitting on a one-acre parcel of land. My offer provided for a ninety-day escrow period. My plan was to get a tentative split of the parcel into four separate lots, with a house on each lot. I would then find a buyer for one of the parcels. I would use the cash generated from the one sale as the required cash down payment on the entire property. The sale of the individual parcel was set up contingent upon two factors:

1. My escrow closing (after all, I couldn't sell something I didn't own)

2. That I could obtain a lot split

In this case, it didn't work, as the local county planning department elected to delay matters until I lost the deal. The true empire builder doesn't lament or dwell on failures. He uses them as a foundation for future success. After all, Thomas Edison failed in his efforts to invent the incandescent light bulb over ten thousand times; those failures provided the necessary experience for his final success. Use your failures as stepping stones to more complete efforts.

The Super Double Escrow Deals

I have a friend who tied up a one-hundred-acre piece of land for six months with a one-hundred-eighty-day escrow. He got a parcel split and was able to arrange the sale of a fifty-acre parcel to a new buyer within the escrow period.

The great part of the deal was that my friend received enough cash from the sale of the fifty acres to pay the remaining fifty acres off totally. It was free and clear of all loans—all with no down payment.

Do you still think that you need money to create wealth? Seize upon opportunity with your creative ideas; you will unlock all the wealth you will ever need.

Formula #67 *Unlocking the Property's Hidden Internal Assets*

Buy a large piece of land that has natural resources on it, such as timber, gold, silver, copper, oil, coal, water, etc. During a long escrow period, arrange to sell some of the natural resources or the rights to them. Use the cash received from this sale for the required cash down payment.

Gary Creates Wealth from an Idea

Gary arranged to buy a large parcel of timberland. Part of the land was rugged and mountainous, but ripe with timber; the other portion of the land was farm ground. Gary really only wanted the farm ground. He had very little cash, but a lot of ideas.

By the time escrow was due to close, Gary had arranged to sell enough timber off the mountainous portion of land to pay off the bottom, more desirable, farmland. He had convinced the seller to put the entire loan against the mountainous land, as the property was divided into two parcels. In return, Gary would make a large cash reduction in the overall loan balance.

Where did Gary get the cash for the down payment and the loan reduction? From the sale of the timber. *He used the hidden internal assets of the property to acquire it.*

Gary did not want to keep the mountainous land. He sold it for a low down payment to a survivalist from the city. The survivalist assumed Gary's debt. This left Gary with a free-and-clear parcel of desirable farmland.

It is time you began looking at property in new and unique ways. Try to find hidden value in it! Then use that value to buy the property. If you can't find value, then it is up to you to create it. Do it today!

Formula #68 *Sweat Escrow*

You might enter an escrow with the following provision: Buyer has the right to perform work on the property during the escrow period.

Mr. Seller should agree to this. After all, you are improving his property. Should you not go through with the deal, he should have a more valuable piece of real estate.

My friend Bryan used this technique recently. He arranged to close escrow on a house deal in ninety days. The purchase price was $30,000 with a $3,000 down payment. The house was a real junker, and Bryan had one minor problem: He didn't have $3,000.

However, Bryan, being a creative empire builder, figured that if he did some minor cosmetic work to the house such as painting, cleaning, etc., he could get a new loan appraisal of $40,000. With a $40,000 appraisal, Bryan figured it would be quite easy to get a $3,000 second mortgage from his local loan broker. Bryan did all the required cosmetic work himself; he got the $3,000 and closed the transaction.

The delayed close, in combination with a little sweat on Bryan's part, allowed him to buy a nice rental house for no down payment.

Formula #69   Credits

Use the rental deposits, owner's impound accounts, and prorations of rents to fund your cash down payment. This technique is commonly used by the real estate pros. If a seller has a surplus impound balance with his lender, negotiate so that money becomes yours. The impound account is generally money set aside to pay taxes and insurance. In many instances, you can request that the lender release those monies to you and that you become responsible for your own tax and insurance payments. These monies could be released in escrow to help fund your cash requirements to close a deal.

Rental Deposits

When you buy rental property, make sure that any deposits that tenants may have made are transferred to you in escrow. These funds might serve as a significant credit toward reducing your cash down payment.

For example, let's say you are buying a four-unit building and each tenant has a $250 security deposit on his apartment. When deposits are transferred in escrow, you would get (4 x 250 =) $1,000 credit or direct reduction in the amount of the cash you might have to come up with to close escrow. That is a significant amount of money, if you are operating on the Conservation of Cash Philosophy: Always conserve cash.

CLOSING DATES CAN MEAN CASH

The date of closing is also significant. Generally, you will find that first payments on notes that you have assumed or on financing the owner is carrying back are due in thirty days after escrow closes. If you close escrow at the beginning of the month, let's say the first, then you can request that the seller collect all rents for that month and deposit them in escrow. This will be a credit to your side of the escrow, and it will again further reduce your cash required to close. Since you get a credit now and your first payment is not due for thirty days, how do you make the payment when it is due? It's good ol' rent collection time again.

The escrow period and Mr. R.E. Agent offer some unique opportunities to reduce and in some cases totally eliminate the need for a cash down payment. I must repeat: These formulas are only a few of the innumerable combinations that a lively imagination can create. The only limitation to solving cash down payment problems are those that you place on your own imagination. Take positive action today!

CHAPTER 13
The Government Helps Everybody

When you were growing up, did you have a favorite aunt
or uncle who would give you anything you asked for—
candy, gum, money, etc.? If you did not have a favorite

aunt or uncle who gave these things to you, you have been cheated! It is your birthright! Hasn't anyone ever told you about Uncle Sam?

Uncle Sam, through our friendly government agencies, has been filling empty outstretched hands for many years. If you need, Uncle Sam will print money to fill that need. Uncle Sam feels that certain things are given in life. One of these givens is affordable housing for all. Our uncle wants each and every one of us to be homeowners. Homeowners make happy citizens. In fact, if you know how to play his bureaucratic game, he might even give you a home of your own—for free.

I know that you are anxious to meet your philanthropic uncle, so let's find out how he is going to help you buy your dream home.

FHA PROGRAM

The Federal Housing Administration is an agency in Uncle Sam's house that insures mortgages that private institutional lenders make. FHA guarantees that if Mr. Savings and Loan has to foreclose, any loss sustained will be covered by the federal government.

Formula #70   Uncle Sam's Guarantee

The owner-occupied FHA loan program is really quite a blessing to the budding homeowner. Currently, the amount that you can borrow on an FHA-guaranteed loan goes as high as $142,650, depending on the part of the country you buy in and what type of property you buy. The good news is that your cash down payment is only three percent on the first $25,000 of the acquisition cost and five percent on the rest of the price above $25,000. On a $75,000 house, then, the down payment requirement would be:

$$
\begin{array}{lll}
\text{First } \$25,000 \times 3\% & = & \$\ \ 750 \\
\text{Remaining } \$50,000 \times 5\% & = & \underline{\ \ 2,500} \\
& & \$3,250
\end{array}
$$

The buyer does pay a fee that goes into an insurance fund. Out of this fund, Uncle Sam bails out lenders who have to foreclose on FHA-guaranteed properties.

Of course, you still need to come up with the small cash down payment; but come on—if you've been asleep and have just been holding this book on your lap, I'm sure that you can still come up with an idea or two for generating this cash.

These loans are not all peaches and cream. They take a long time to process, which can jeopardize the super deal that must be closed quickly; and, the seller generally has to pay points. Points are a percentage of the loan amount. One point generally refers to one percent of the loan amount. In a seller's market, it is hard to get a seller to stand still for the time it takes to close these loans and the cost of points. If they do wait, you can generally be sure that you're paying a high retail price for the house (unless it is a buyer's market).

Now the good news! FHA has been fairly lenient in terms of what can be used for a down payment. They have been known to approve cars, boats, or other personal property in lieu of a cash down payment. Uncle Sam understands barter!

The real gold mine comes because old FHA loans are fully assumable. Many of these long-term, relatively low-interest, fixed-rate loans are what the successful empire builder must search out and find in the real estate market of the eighties. (We are going to talk more about the importance of these loans in a later chapter.)

Formula #71 *No Down Payment in Rural Areas*

The Farmers Home Administration, or FmHA, is an agency similar to FHA. FmHA's primary function is to promote homeownership in the rural areas of our country.

I had some tenants—Tom and Kelly—who, like many young people today, were discouraged about their homeownership dream. Tom and Kelly just could not seem to save the required cash for a down payment for buying their own home.

They heard about the FmHA program and investigated it. They discovered that if a qualified property was found they could get in for no cash down payment through a FmHA financing program.

They found a brand-new house in a desirable neighborhood and proceeded to buy their first home. Their total cash outlay: nothing—all with Uncle Sam's FmHA help!

They did have to show a good credit and income history. But if Uncle Sam thinks that no down payment is a reasonable way to buy property, then you can be assured that it is not such a radical departure from conventional real estate wisdom.

Formula #72   The VA Opportunity

The Veterans Administration (VA) is another benevolent outstretched hand of Uncle Sam. In this program, the VA fully guarantees the loan in case of default.

In this program, you do not have to come up with any down payment. If you are a veteran, just waltz into the Veterans Administration Office with holes in your pockets, and your kindly uncle might be willing to guarantee a real estate loan up to $100,000.

You do have to initially occupy the home, and woe is you if you buy a house under a VA guarantee and do not move into it. It is a federal crime!

However, if you move into the house and at some future date decide to move again, that should be okay. You might even get to use another VA-guaranteed loan. Talk to your local VA office for more details.

Formula #73   The $1 House

The government is literally giving away houses in inner city areas throughout the country for one dollar—that's right, one dollar! You might assume an existing low-interest loan, or Uncle Sam might make available a new subsidized low-interest loan.

This program was designed by HUD (Department of Housing and Urban Development) for the cities of our nation in an effort to attract middle-income people back to the inner city. In fact, Uncle Sam is even willing to arrange low-interest loans for the fix-up work.

You do have to live in the property until the house is fixed up. However, once the rehab work is done, you are free to sell it, rent, or do whatever you want with the property. Talk to your local HUD office or city government for more of the details. If you don't mind living in the inner city, check into this no down payment bonanza today—another no down payment formula brought to you by your friendly Uncle Sam.

Formula #74   FHA and VA Repossessions

FHA and VA foreclosures are great sources of obtaining one hundred percent financing on a deal. Because of the marginal buyers that these two agencies sometimes guarantee, the incidence of default is fairly high when compared to conventional loans.

FHA and VA repossessions are quite common. Some real estate brokers handle these situations almost exclusively. Before reselling these houses, the law says that they need to be fixed up. Uncle Sam many times puts in more money, cashwise, to rehab a property than he gets back as a cash down payment when they're resold.

Check with your local HUD office and find out if you can help solve Uncle Sam's property problems by buying FHA or HUD foreclosures with one hundred percent financing. Also check with the Veterans Administration; you will find some high-leverage foreclosure buys here if you can stomach all the red tape.

GET TO KNOW FANNIE MAE

The Federal National Mortgage Association (FNMA, also referred to as Fannie Mae) is a quasi-government corporation formed to buy large pools of loans from banks, savings and loans, and other mortgage companies. In years past, when interest rates were low, Fannie Mae acquired lots of loans with interest rates of only seven to ten percent. Unfortunately, the cost Fannie Mae had to pay in the bond markets exceeded what their yield was on these old low-interest loans. They found themselves in a bit of a dilemma. They were paying more for the money than they were receiving.

Never fear, innovative companies always know that solutions are near. Fannie Mae designed an appealing and creative refinance program for property owners who have these low-interest-rate loans. When properties with these loans are sold, Fannie Mae will provide a new ninety-five percent loan to the value. For refinancing, you may be able to get as much as ninety percent of the property's value. To find out whether the loan on your house (or prospective house) was sold to Fannie Mae, call the lender or check the county courthouse for the name of the beneficiary.

Formula #75   *Fannie Mae Refinance*

A no down payment transaction is relatively easy using Fannie Mae loans. Let's assume that you've found an $80,000 house. The seller owes $25,000 on the first mortgage. The seller needs at least $45,000 cash to buy his new dream home. He is even willing to carry back a note for the balance of his equity. Have the seller refinance his house with the Fannie Mae program at ninety percent of the value. Ninety percent of $80,000 is $72,000. With the $72,000, the seller would pay off his old $25,000 loan. Of course, $72,000 minus $25,000 leaves $47,000 cash remaining. Let's say that $2,000 would go for loan costs, so the seller would be left with his $45,000 in cash.

If the seller was responsible for the loan costs (this is negotiable) his carryback note would be $8,000. This note would be given by you and secured by a second mortgage on the property. The seller is happy because, with the $45,000, he can buy his new dream house. You are delighted because you've just acquired the house without a dime of your own money.

The interesting part about this Fannie Mae program is that the lender may blend the old rate of interest with current rates and give you a compromised interest rate.

For example, if the current loan on your property carries an eight percent interest rate and current rates are at thirteen percent, the lender might loan you the proceeds at a rate somewhere between eleven and twelve percent. This compromise rate of interest is an incentive to encourage you to retire that old loan.

CHAPTER 14
The Prince and the Pauper: Partnerships

What do you do when you have found that super deal of the year? You start brainstorming, and your creative juices are sizzling. You negotiate long and hard with the seller, but he still says, "I need $20,000 cash and that's the final word."

You don't have $20,000 cash. Your line of credit at the bank is stretched to its limit. You become discouraged, thinking that you're going to let such a super deal slip right through your hands.

But wait! The dynamic real estate empire builder is a problem solver. There must be a solution! Perhaps a partnership is the answer.

Formula #76   The Limited Partnership

Raise the necessary cash to close a super deal by forming a limited partnership.

About one and a half years ago, I was looking at some apartment units in the Lake Tahoe area of California. I had driven by these units many times over the period of a year. During that time, I had noticed the "For Sale" sign, and that the units were looking more run-down each time I drove by.

I called the sales agent. She told me that the asking price was $195,000 with a $65,000 down payment. Mrs. Agent added, "The sellers might be flexible—they really want out."

The price and terms did seem a little stiff for my program at the time, but, if the sellers really wanted out badly enough, I figured that I might be able to help. I made an appointment to see the units.

The units had approximately $10,000 in deferred maintenance, and after looking over the books, it appeared that there was a chronic management problem associated with the building. It just wasn't being run efficiently.

I made the following offer:

- Price: $140,000

- Down payment: $10,000

- Owner to carry back a note for $130,000 at ten percent interest with a balloon payment due in three years; payments would be payable monthly at interest only.

The agent was certain that the offer wouldn't be accepted . . . which is probably why it wasn't. Through negotiations that lasted more than three weeks and included several counter offers, we finally agreed on the following price and terms:

- Price: $150,000

- Down payment: $20,000

- Owner to carry back a note for $130,000 at twelve percent interest with a balloon payment due in two years. (From now on, no more two-year balloons; they're too dangerous.)

The accepted offer was made subject to the approval of my partners. What partners? I didn't have any partners. But you can bet that for a super deal like this, I would find partners.

I figured that the property was worth about $175,000 in "as is" condition—that is, without any fix-up work. It was a nice deal. Now all I needed was the money to close it.

I did know a few people who had expressed an interest in real estate investments in the past. They had the cash, and I had the deal and the know-how.

I offered various percentages of the potential profit to a number of investors. I would keep fifty percent for my efforts. If I find the deal and offer to manage it, that is generally the least compensation I will accept. Of course, I won't present an average deal to prospective partners, only the super ones.

The investors were definitely interested! We formed a limited partnership. I was the general, or managing, partner. The investors were the limited partners. (Work with a competent real estate attorney to draft the necessary contract when forming partnerships, at least for the first couple of times).

Basically, the limited partnership came down to this:

- The investors put up $20,000 cash to close the deal and $10,000 cash to take care of the fix-up work.

- I would coordinate the fix-up work, supervise the existing manager, take care of the bookkeeping, and generally be responsible for the overall project.

- When the project was sold, the limited partners would receive their original investment back first; we would then split the remaining profit fifty-fifty after all costs were paid.

One year after our purchase, we sold the units for $205,000. It was an all-cash sale. After commissions, closing costs, and other incidentals, the investors received all their original cash investment back plus a fifty percent annual rate of return . . . not bad, for a passive investor. By using the Conservation of Capital Philosophy—by using other people's money—I made over $16,000 from that little transaction as my portion of the profit.

The investors were happy! In fact, several of them wanted to jump back into the real estate market with me again. You develop faithful partners by being successful. This was truly a win-win situation for all.

The limited partnership is only one of many ways a partnership or a group can invest in real estate. Let's take a look at some of the other ways:

- Joint venture

- General partnership

- Subchapter S corporation

- Corporation

- Real Estate Investment Trust

Discuss the alternatives available with a good real estate attorney; ask the attorney which type of group ownership would be best for your particular personal and financial situation.

Formula #77   *Partnership and Discounting*

Form a partnership to buy mortgages, trust deeds, gemstones, currency land, etc., at a large discount; then exchange these items at full retail value into real estate.

You provide the idea and organizing ability—your partners provide the cash.

Formula #78   The Partnership Cash Cranker

Do you need to raise some cash to close a transaction? Form a partnership and sell an interest in another one of your properties to raise the necessary cash.

Make sure that you base the sales price on a realistic appraisal. No blue sky here! You are just bargaining for future trouble if you sell to the partnership at an artificially inflated price. This is an excellent source for raising cash quickly, particularly once you have a track record.

Formula #79   The Partner's Financial Statement

Use a partner's financial statement. If you need institutional financing, but your credit smells and you have a feeble financial statement, find a financially strong partner. Have him get the loan in his name, or cosign one for you. He might initially buy the property, and after escrow closes he could deed the property or a portion of it back to you. What are some of the incentives you might give a partner?

- Part ownership

- Sharing the appreciation profits

- Money

- A dream

- A note

- A service (mow his lawn for five years; whatever it takes)

Formula #80   Syndicated Partnership Option

The syndicated option is a powerful investment tool that can generate the cash necessary to tie up a promising piece of real estate.

You've come upon a tract of land in the path of growth. You approach Mr. Owner about an option. Mr. Owner says, "Sure, I'll give you an option to buy my property for two years, but I want $25,000 cash as option money."

You are fairly certain that this land will increase in value over the next couple of years; but still, you are very aware that options may be hazardous to your pocketbook if you guess wrong . . . they are risky!

You decide to form a partnership to raise the cash to buy the option. By getting several people involved, you spread the risk of a possible total loss of the $25,000. Also, the partners put up the cash and your risk is only the time invested.

You offer the deal to five high-income investors. Each contributes $5,000. You get fifty percent of any of the profits that occur if you have guessed right. The investors split the other fifty percent.

Be sure to clearly spell out the risks involved in such a venture to the investors. They need to understand that they could make a significant return on their investment or lose it all entirely.

There are many high-income people for whom this is an acceptable risk within their investment portfolio. Find them and try this technique.

WHERE DO YOU FIND PARTNERS?

Try asking family members first. Approach a family member who has money in a passbook savings account or any low-yield taxable savings plan. Ask them if they know what inflation is doing to the purchasing power of their money.

You bet they know—sort of! Show them on paper an easy-to-understand analysis of what inflation is doing to their money. A simple analysis might go like this: "Uncle Thrifty, you have $20,000 in the bank and you are earning seven percent interest. That gives you ($7\% \times \$20,000 =$) $1,400 a year in interest.

"That doesn't sound bad for a safe, secure investment. But wait, you are in the twenty-eight percent tax bracket, aren't you? That means that Uncle Sam gets ($28\% \times \$1,400 =$) $392 of your interest. That leaves you with $1,008 after taxes as the real return on the savings account."

You might add, "Uncle Thrifty, do you know that your effective after-tax yield is only about five percent?"

He might counter, "Yes, but at least it is safe and

secure, and I know that I won't lose it in some risky deal."

You might say, "Did you know that the inflation rate is running at about four percent annually? Therefore you're really only earning one percent on your savings account. If inflation increases, the purchasing power of your money is guaranteed to go downhill. That is not secure, it is a low-return investment in grave danger of becoming a losing one."

A simple analysis of this type is impressive to most people. Family members may still see you as an irresponsible child, a dreamer, a bum, a spaced-out hippy, etc. Your job is to change that image, to show them how responsible and competent you have become. You need to show them how more money can be made and kept in a real estate partnership with you than in their present investment program.

Professional and Business People

People you know in the professional and business community are a good source of partnership funds. Your doctor, dentist, or chiropractor may have some spare cash for investment. This person might be the ideal passive investor. He works long hours, makes lots of money, and does not have a lot of time to devote to outside investments.

The one reservation I have about using doctors as investors is that they are constantly being approached by people touting various investment schemes, so that you may not find them receptive to listening to your presentation. Most doctors (most people) do not have the skills to discriminate between a good investment and a bad one even if it jumped up and bit them on the nose.

The key to attracting any partner is to casually mention what you are doing. You might want to go over the simple inflation analysis approach used with the family. Drop figures like expected yield from the real estate investment; make sure that you can stand behind the yields that you mention.

Above all, do not beg! Arrange the presentation so that

the investor is convinced that he or she needs you. After all, the investor does need you. You are providing a valuable service. Do not sell yourself short! If you have a truly promising real estate investment, the money will seek you out!

Lawyers, accountants, and other business people are a fertile source for potential partners. These people are very interested in the nuts and bolts analysis of the investment; tax benefits, after-tax yield, what happens if something goes wrong? The business-oriented person generally has an ability to analyze the facts and come to an independent decision.

Other Prospective Partners

The following represents a list of people who might be approached as prospective investors in your partnerships:

- Financial planners
- Insurance agents
- Loan brokers
- Politicians
- Business executives
- Judges
- Engineers
- Jewelers
- Sellers
- Real estate agents and brokers
- Stockbrokers and security dealers

Make sure that you have a clearly written financial analysis (tax, projected yields, demographics of location, neighborhood). If you have not done your homework, these people will put you out the door quickly.

Relax, the financial analysis and prospectus is not as difficult to put together as it might appear.

The Prospectus and Financial Analysis

Whether you are soliciting funds from family, friends, or professional and business people, you need to prepare a prospectus. This prospectus will lay out the details of the transaction: financial, contractual, security, etc.

If you do not feel comfortable computing figures, have an accountant or a capable friend help you with the first couple of deals.

DEALING WITH PARTNERS

Let's take a look at some of the rules an empire builder will want to follow to ensure that successful and profitable partnerships are formed.

1. Do not beg! As an empire builder, you have the most important assets: ideas and ambition. You are proposing to solve the investor's problem—where will he invest his depreciating dollars? See yourself as successful; be positive and confident. Calmly exude the attitude that, "Mr. Investor, you need me more than I need you."

2. Choose your partners very carefully! I cannot emphasize this enough. Find people with whom you can get along personally. The biggest mistake a beginning empire builder makes in this area is to be so thoroughly excited about the project that he takes the first investor who comes along, whether he is compatible or not. This is a critical error.

People normally are the root of distress sale situations, not property. An incompatible partnership can turn a super deal into a distress sale.

A bad partner is one who calls you too much, suspects every move you make, and generally cultivates an air of nervousness and distrust. This won't work! Compatibility in a partnership is essential. If the partnership turns sour, split as soon as possible and don't look back.

3. Define your agreement clearly in writing! One of the biggest sources of misunderstanding in partnerships has to do with what I call the "vague—I am sure" memory syndrome. One partner distinctly remembers something concerning the original agreement, while another partner conveniently forgets it.

Don't be a flake! Clearly write down all facets of the partnership agreement to avoid future misunderstandings.

4. Make it understood at the outset that it is an equal partnership—but you are the managing partner. Let there be no doubt as to who has the investment skills and who is directly responsible for the day-to-day activities.

That doesn't mean that you should ignore a partner's advice. Listen and learn; but it is absolutely vital that you take charge. Your partner wants to know that you have total command of the project and his money.

5. Try not to invest any of your own money into the partnership. The empire builder's contributions to the partnership are ideas and energy, his ability to find and negotiate that super deal. Do not underestimate that value.

6. Protect your partner's interests at all costs. If you find that you have made an error in judgment due to incomplete research on your part, save the partner's investment to the total exclusion of your interest.

For instance, say that after closing escrow, you learn that an oil refinery is going to be built right behind the new investment house you just bought with a partner. "No wonder I got such a good deal on it," you say.

Act quickly to sell, exchange, or sue your way out of the problem as soon as possible. Let Mr. Partner know what has happened right away. Share the bad news as well as the good with Mr. Partner. He will appreciate your forthrightness and honesty. It will help you in the long run in attracting acceptable investors to your program.

Never sit down and mumble the bad news to a partner and then attempt to skip over it.

7. Qualify investors before you enter a partnership. Sit down and listen to their financial, professional, and personal goals. Find out what their income is. Are you taking their last dime to buy this property? I always attempt to choose partners who have other reserve funds in case of an emergency.

If, through discussion, you find that Mr. Investor needs his money back in two years and you are looking at a five-year investment program, you may find a conflict. Resolve that conflict before you form the partnership.

Partnerships are a lot like marriage. We sometimes run into them blindly and suffer untold pain as a result. However, if you follow the guidelines set down in this chapter, you will find partnerships a powerful way in which to accelerate your progress toward building a real estate empire.

Overcome your fear today. Find the property first. When you find that super deal, partners will be lined up to get a piece of the action.

CHAPTER 15
Accelerated and Combination Financing

Recently, I heard about a guy who would not buy a property unless, at the close of escrow, he walked away with cash in his pocket. This is no misprint. Each time he buys an investment house, he gets paid for it. He walks away from the title company with cash in his pocket.

As long as he is getting paid for it, he can continue buying indefinitely. Not a bad combination, getting the benefits of real estate ownership and a paycheck for doing what he loves to do.

Let's look at some of the formulas that will put cash in your pocket from buying real estate instead of selling it.

Formula #81   *The Subordination*

Mr. Mortgage Holder *subordinates* his collateral position so that a new mortgage can be placed on the property.

I was fortunate enough to find the circumstances in which I could use the magic of the *subordination clause* in one of the first deals I did. I actually stumbled into the situation without any real knowledge of what I was doing.

I was approached by a fellow who desperately wanted to sell a rental house. He needed to sell in order to pay off some debts. He wanted $17,000. My wife and I had rented this house two years before, so we were quite familiar with it. I figured that the house was worth at least $26,000, so his asking price was extremely low.

I was just getting familiar with real estate, its terminology, financing, the market, etc., so at first I thought the low price might be a warning signal that something could be wrong with the house or the deal. After all, I knew that this fellow owned more property than anybody else in town. Everybody knew what a shrewd businessman he was; but I soon discovered that even a shrewd businessman's judgment can crumble under debt pressure. I checked into the deal with more thoroughness than necessary. Everything seemed okay with the house and the transaction, so I moved ahead!

I discovered that this fellow wanted the following kind of offer:

Buyer assumes 1st trust deed	$ 2,100
Buyer assumes 2nd trust deed	4,900
Buyer's cash down payment	10,000
Total Price	$17,000

I went to the local savings and loan and applied for a loan that represented eighty percent of the value of the property. Mr. M., the loan officer, asked me what I thought the property was worth. I told him $26,000 to $28,000. He said that he would do an appraisal and get back to me.

I stopped by to check on the progress of my loan application a few days later. Mr. M. said, "The appraisal only came in at $26,500."

I thought to myself, "That's okay, I only need $17,000."

Then Mr. M. dropped a bombshell: "Ed, I'm sorry, but we can only loan you $21,200 on the house."

At first I thought, "Great! After all, $17,000 is all I need." After I left Mr. M., I got to thinking. What would happen if I took the $21,200 loan and paid Mr. V. $17,000? Would the remainder of the cash go to the seller? Closing costs couldn't be that much! In my ignorance, I was confused.

Then a light went on in my head. I could finance the property for more than I would pay for it, and put the extra cash in my pocket.

I began feeling guilty about my good fortune. I thought that maybe I was doing something wrong. I went to Mr. M. and told him, "I'm only paying $17,000 for the property. Do I get the extra $4,200 at the close of escrow?"

"Of course not," he said in a rather disturbed tone of voice. "There must have been an error in the appraisal."

He finally agreed to loan me $15,000 on the house. I was disappointed, because I had been sure that I could get one hundred percent financing on the house. I didn't have $2,000 to close the deal.

Then an idea came to me . . . not *cash*, but an *idea*. The idea referred to something I'd read in William Nickerson's book, *How I Turned $1,000 into $3,000,000 in Real Estate in My Spare Time*. That idea was subordination.

Subordination is a process where an existing noteholder agrees to let you place a new loan on a property, and the existing noteholder would allow his lien to come behind the new loan in the event of default.

This is how I used the subordination clause.

I went to the holder of the second trust deed on the

house. I asked him if he would subordinate his $4,900 loan and allow me to place a new first trust deed on my property. If he would do that, I would agree to raise the interest rate on his note from eight percent to nine percent. He readily agreed.

Here is a recap of what finally happened:

New first trust deed	$15,000 @ 9%, 20 yrs @ 138.72 mo.	
Subordinated second T.D.	$ 4,900 @ 9% int. only @ 36.75 mo.	
	Due in 10 yrs.	
	TOTAL PAYMENT	$175.47
Loan proceeds		$19,900
Purchase price		17,000
Net cash to me		$ 2,900

I was able to rent the house for $210 per month. Mr. Tenant made my debt service and covered the taxes and insurance payments. I got $2,900 cash at the close of escrow, a tax shelter, and a rapidly appreciating investment house.

Just think, I got all these benefits because of one idea: subordination. If I hadn't been exposed to and pursued that idea, I might have passed on a super deal. How many super deals have you passed on because you lacked solutions? The idea that you can turn real estate problems into cash in your pocket is waiting for you.

This book is designed to give you ideas that you'll need to solve your real estate empire building problems; start using and applying these ideas in your life today.

Formula #82 *Share the Wealth*

Have Mr. Seller refinance the property and you share in the cash proceeds. Mr. Seller might then take back the remainder of his equity in a subordinated carryback note.

For example, Mr. Seller is asking $60,000 for his house. He owes $25,000. Have him refinance his house for $48,000. Out of the $48,000, he will have to pay off the $25,000 existing loan; that leaves him with $23,000 cash. You make your offer subject to him getting $15,000 cash and you getting $8,000 cash. Mr. Seller could then carry back a second trust deed for $20,000. You share a little bit of the wealth and get the property; Mr. Seller gets some cash, a note, and out from under the mortgage obligations (if you agree to assume the loans).

Mr. Seller is willing to do this, because he has had the house for sale for several months. He is very motivated. Let's recap the transaction.

- Total purchase price: $60,000

- Total loans: first, $48,000 plus second, $20,000 = $68,000

- You get approximately $8,000 cash at the close of escrow

- Mr. Seller gets $15,000 cash

You have successfully overfinanced or over-collateralized the property, i.e., the loans on the property exceed the property's value. This is a neat way to buy property and raise cash. Be careful and make sure that you can handle the debt load.

Jim H.'s Overfinance Success

I know a guy named Jim. Jim successfully used this formula to pull cash out of over twenty houses in a one-month period.

Jim bought almost $1,000,000 worth of houses and was able to put almost $75,000 cash in his pocket at the close of escrow. He did this all in one month using this one simple idea.

The most essential factor in making this technique work is finding a real live Mr. Motivation and solving his problem.

Generally, this works best with properties with large equities and a seller who desperately needs cash.

During negotiations, it is a good idea to point out and explain the flimsy security position of the seller's note. Make sure that Mr. Seller signs a document saying that he

understands the financing arrangement and agrees to it.
"An ounce of prevention . . ."

Formula #83   *Share the Wealth with a Created Note*

A variation on the last formula might work like this:
Create a note secured by another piece of property that
you own. Mr. Seller might feel more comfortable that
way, particularly if you have an equity cushion in that
property.

Let's say that you have a house that has a value of
$75,000. You owe $45,000 on it. In the previous formula,
the seller took back a $20,000 note secured by the prop-
erty. Some sellers might object to that arrangement because of the lack of security for the note.

If you meet with that objection, try giving Mr. Seller a
$30,000 note secured by another piece of property. This
might give the seller more security, depending on the
equity in the property. You might even be in a better
position to ask for more cash out of escrow—a bigger
paycheck because of a little twist to an idea.

I know a couple of guys who use this formula a couple
times a month. Not a bad way of creating cash flow,
is it?

Formula #84   *The Personal Note Cranker*

Find a free-and-clear house and give the seller your
personal note for the equity. After escrow closes, arrange
to have a new loan put on the property and put that cash
in your pocket. You will have just traded your personal
note for cash.

A variation on this idea might include giving Mr. Seller
a deferred cash down payment along with your personal
note. You could then close the deal and get a new loan.
From the new loan proceeds you could pay off the deferred cash down payment.

Jerry Turns his Note to Cash

I have a friend named Jerry. He found a free-and-clear
house that looked like a good buy. The owner was asking

$80,000. Jerry offered the owner $10,000 down and his personal note for the balance, which was $70,000. He offered to pay the note off at $510.23 per month, including eight percent interest, amortized over a thirty-year period. The owner accepted.

After taking title, Jerry put a new loan on the property for $60,000. He received that cash to do with as he pleased—to invest, go to Tahiti, buy a new car, etc. Of course, Jerry, being a dynamic empire builder, reinvested this money in real estate. He understood how money quickly compounds itself into millions, if invested properly.

Did Mr. Seller get taken to the cleaners? No, I don't think so! Mr. Seller felt secure with Jerry's personal note. He knew that Jerry had other property and assets. If a default occurred, Mr. Seller could probably get a court judgment against Jerry and all of his assets. He could place a lien on all Jerry's properties. The seller felt this was almost equal to getting a blanket mortgage on all of Jerry's properties.

Jerry traded his personal note for cash. Mr. Seller got what he felt was blanket security for his note. Both ended up winners.

OTHER CREATIVE COMBINATIONS

Formula #85 The Gemstone Combinations

Buy gemstones such as rubies, sapphires, and diamonds at wholesale value. Find a Mr. Motivation and trade the gemstones to him at retail value for his property

After escrow closes, place a new loan on the property. Use the cash generated from the refinance proceeds to pay off your supplier of gemstones; if you've got a healthy markup on the gemstones, there should be plenty of cash left over for you to put a nice profit in your pocket.

Paul F. Masters this Formula

My friend Paul is a master of this technique of using gemstones. He has a wholesale source for investment grade diamonds. Paul can buy these diamonds for approximately thirty-three percent of their retail appraised value.

Recently, Paul became interested in the following house:

Offering price		$100,000
Loans		-0-
	Equity	$100,000

He made the following offer:

$100,000	Full price offer
25,000	Cash down payment to be deferred for ninety days after the close of escrow.
50,000	Retail value of diamonds
25,000	Seller carries back a note and trust deed that will subordinate to a new first trust deed

After escrow closes, Paul puts a new loan on the property for $75,000. He pays the following people out of the cash received from the new loan:

Seller's deferred down payment	$25,000
Diamond supplier's payment	16,000
(Remember, Paul bought these at wholesale)	
Costs of obtaining the loan	1,400
	$43,000

Paul receives	$75,000
He pays out	43,000
Net cash in his pocket	$32,000

This little idea yielded Paul $32,000 cash. In addition, he still owns the property. He was doing one of these a month the last time I talked to him. Paul's accelerating the growth of his empire . . . it's time for you to start yours.

Formula #86 Prepayment Discount

Find Mr. Motivation who needs cash. He might be willing to sell his property at a significant discount, if he can get all cash. Make the following deal with Mr. Motivation, using a *prepayment discount* clause in the note. The formula would work like this:

- Offering price: $75,000

- Mr. Motivation gets a new loan for $40,000

- Mr. Motivation carries back a long-term $20,000 second trust deed with the following provision in it: "If the trustor pays the note off in one year, the beneficiary agrees to discount the note fifty percent from its face value."

- Mr. Motivation also carries back a third trust deed for $15,000. In this trust deed, there is a subordination clause so that the buyer can put a new second trust deed on the property at a future date.

- After escrow closes, you arrange a new second trust deed for $20,000.

- You pay off Mr. Motivation's second T.D., which has the fifty percent discount off the $20,000 face value of the note; he would receive $10,000 cash.

- You keep the other $10,000 cash and the property.

Formula #87 Line of Credit plus Fix-up

Combine any of the "Pulling Money Out of a Hat" formulas with institutional or seller financing.

I know a couple of guys who have made their million in real estate with only this one simple formula. They find a rental house for, let's say, $75,000. It is in need of some minor repair: cosmetic improvements such as new carpets, new drapes, paint, etc.

My friends might figure that once the cosmetic work has been done, the house will fetch $95,000 on the market. They borrow $10,000 from their bank. (They have established a good line of credit with their banker.) They use $7,500 for the down payment on the house and the other $2,500 for the cosmetic improvements.

After all the work is completed, they generally get a new loan on the property based on the increased value. With the refinance cash proceeds they pay off Mr. Banker and move on to another deal. Without cash coming out of their pocket they can continue to buy indefinitely.

Formula #88   Land Advance

The contractor's land advance is a technique used by savvy builders all the time. It works like this: Mr. Contractor ties up a lot or parcel of land with an earnest money agreement. Then Mr. Contractor asks Mr. Banker for a land advance to pay off the loan on the lot in preparation for him building a house. This would all be part of the construction loan.

The land advance monies could go for paying off the entire lot, or the seller of the lot could agree to subordinate part of the value of his note by allowing you only a partial paydown of a note. This could put some extra cash in Mr. Contractor's pocket. Mr. Contractor gets one hundred percent financing using the land advance technique.

OVERCOME YOUR LIMITATIONS

When I first started thinking about investing in real estate, my ideas for buying were fairly simple and straightforward. I thought that a minimum down payment for any house was $4,000, with the bank financing the rest. If the transaction didn't happen the way I imagined it should— because Mr. Banker said that I didn't qualify—or I didn't have the cash down payment—well, I was prepared to give up the deal. Does that sound familiar? By accepting that there was basically only one way to make a deal, I had unknowingly placed a giant set of limitations on my ability to create. I went to my local savings and loan manager inquiring about a loan to buy this nice rental house. Mr. M., the manager, decided to give me some free advice. "Don't buy that house, Ed. Repair costs will eat you alive, management will give you ulcers, and you just cannot make money in today's real estate market." (This happened in 1976.)

Mr. M. had deflated my newfound enthusiasm. After all, he was an experienced businessman. He must know what he was talking about.

I allowed Mr. M. to impose his limitations on my life. He was really saying to me, "I couldn't make money in real estate, because I don't choose to try . . . so you shouldn't try, either."

When I left Mr. M., I was depressed. I went home and began to review some of my real estate reading material and the basic facts concerning the investment house. The facts convinced me that the house was still a good investment. I just needed to come up with a few ideas to solve some of the problems. I applied some of the problem-solving techniques in this book.

The idea came! I bought the house and got a loan from Mr. M., despite his tacit disapproval. The deal worked out well and I was able to make thousands of dollars off the property. It worked because I was willing to break through my own limited concepts of how a deal *should* be made, and I didn't allow Mr. M. to impose his limited vision of the world on my circumstances.

You are directly responsible for the circumstances in your life. Do you want to change? Do you want to be rich? You have the power to create the ideas to change your life today. Use that power, that inner determination, to build a financial empire. Take positive action today.

ACCELERATED AND COMBINATION FINANCING

- Define clearly the seller's problem.

- Brainstorm all possible pertinent facts relating to the problem.

- List at least six combinations that will solve real estate problems.

- Rank the solutions in order of desirability.
- Follow through; present it, make the deal work.

CHAPTER 16
Foreclosure Formulas

My friend Don stopped by my office the other day to tell me that he was going to Hawaii for a month. It was August, which is one of the best times of the year for opportunities in real estate transactions, so I asked him, "How can you afford to take off at the height of the busy real estate activity?"

He said, "You know, Ed, I've already made over $200,000 cash in my real estate transactions this year. I don't think I'll work much the rest of the year."

What's Don's secret for generating over $200,000 in cash in less than a single year without using any of his own money? It's the age-old formula at the basis of all fortunes. Don buys properties in foreclosure at well below market prices, and resells them for a substantial profit. Let's see how you can cash in on this bonanza.

FORECLOSURES EQUAL OPPORTUNITY

A foreclosure occurs when the owner of a property fails to meet the conditions set forth in the loan documents on the property. This generally means that loan payments are not current, but it can also include not keeping property in good condition or failure to keep adequate fire insurance on the property. Also, in recent times many properties have been placed in foreclosure because the notes on those properties contained due-on-sale clauses. This meant that the property could not be transferred without permission from the existing noteholder.

Foreclosures are common during economic recessions or when interest rates are high. In the mid-'80s we have seen an all-time high in foreclosures. This has been due to periods of high interest rates and slow times in certain industries, such as oil and gas. This situation presents an excellent opportunity for real estate investors who know how to buy foreclosures.

How the Foreclosure Process Works

Let's say that because a job loss, abuse of credit cards, family illness, or other emergency, Joe Tardy misses his house payment. If his payment is made to an institutional lender, such as a bank or a savings and loan, they will usually wait until a couple of payments are missed before they file a notice of default with the county recorder. However, they can legally file that notice of default the day after the late period penalty is passed.

After Joe receives a copy of the notice of default, the lender can do nothing else for, usually, about ninety days. (This time period varies from state to state and also depends on whether the note is secured by a mortgage or a deed of trust.) This notice of default is published in the local legal newspaper, which is an excellent source for investors who are prospecting for foreclosure buys.

When the ninety-day notification period expires and Joe still hasn't come up with the back payments owed, the lender has the right to call the entire balance of the loan due at that time. In states that have deeds of trust, Joe might be allowed another month to pay off the loan. If the loan is not paid off during this period (check the time requirements in your own state), Joe's property will be sold at an auction to the bidder who bids the highest figure above the loan amount.

If there are no bids on the property, or if no bids equal or exceed the outstanding loan, the lender takes possession of the property. Even if someone does buy it, in some states Joe has the right to redeem his property for as much as a year following the auction if he can pay an amount equal to the back payments, interest, and some penalty charges. If Joe has no redemption privileges, his property is lost to him.

You can see how motivated Joe becomes as the auction date draws near. His degree of motivation offers you a profit opportunity. I don't mean to sound ruthless, but Joe will lose his property whether you and I exist or not. If we have the knowledge, it becomes our duty to help Joe solve his problem and create a profit for ourselves at the same time. This sets the stage for a truly win-win transaction. I'll show you how this works later in this chapter. Right now, you need to know that there are three primary and distinct areas where an empire builder can profit during the foreclosure process. These are during the notice of default period, at the foreclosure auction, and directly from the banks that have been unable to sell foreclosed property at auction.

AREA ONE: NOTICE OF DEFAULT

During the early stages of this period, the owner's motivation quotient may not be very high. He might be thinking, "I've got three or four months, that's enough time to get a loan from Uncle Stingy or maybe find a good cash buyer at a decent price."

However, as time begins to run short, Mr. Tardy's motivation quotient may skyrocket. This is the time to negotiate the kind of flexible transaction that will allow you to make thousands of dollars on this one deal.

I have found the two-pronged method of contact to be most effective in making successful foreclosure transactions. First, contact the owner by postcard the day the notice of default is filed. Some people panic at their name being published on what might be seen as a "deadbeat list." They might be prepared for a clean, quick transaction.

If you don't get a nibble on the first postcard, another one sent as auction time draws near might reach a person who has become more receptive. The owner now has to do something or face a total loss of equity.

If the owner contacts you, give the impression that you are only mildly interested. Begin to learn the details of the situation by casually asking the following questions:

1. Is title to the property in your name?

2. What is the property address?

3. How would you rate the neighborhood?

4. How much is the loan balance on the property?

5. What are the terms of the loan?

6. Who is the lender?

7. How far behind in payments are you?

8. How much money will it take to bring it current?

9. What is wrong with the house?

10. Why did you fall behind in payments?

11. What is the lowest price you would accept if I gave you an offer today?

12. Who is the trustee foreclosing?

13. Do you have any other judgments, liens, or loans against the property?

14. Is your fire insurance current? Until when?

15. Where will you move when the house is gone?

16. How much time is left before the lender repossesses your home?

After you've asked these questions, if the seller still appears to be motivated to salvage some of his equity and you feel that you can get the property for eighty percent of market value or less, then make an appointment to see the home.

Avoiding the Pitfalls

You're overjoyed with excitement and enthusiasm when you see the property. It appears to be a super deal. Based on the information the seller has given you, you enter into a purchase agreement to buy the house on the spot. Right? Dead wrong! That would be the quickest way I know to lose at the real estate game.

FACT: The seller on a foreclosed piece of property almost never will give you accurate answers with respect to loan balances, other judgments and liens, the property's value, and hidden defects on the property. I don't choose to believe that distressed sellers lie with malicious intent, but somehow the basic facts get distorted. Prior to seeing the seller's house, do your homework. The following will give you some guidance in avoiding future problems.

1. Check out the value of the property. You can do this by checking with local real estate agents and finding several comparable sales in the vicinity of the property in which you are interested. Make sure that you find out the price for which properties actually sold, not just the value on the listing. You could also hire an independent appraiser to give you a good market value. Also, check out what's happening in the neighborhood. Is there anything going on that might increase or decrease property values?

2. Go to the title company or attorney handling the fore-closure and find out exact answers to our foreclosure questionnaire. Pay particular attention to such information as loan amounts, amount needed to bring loan(s) current, other loans, judgments, liens, and the time period remaining before the default period ends. Get a preliminary title report at this time, also.

3. Call the lender and verify the loan balances, assumability of the loan (I have found that lenders will generally allow a new party with good credit, or sometimes even not-so-good credit, to assume a loan in foreclosure without bumping up the interest rate), and the specific terms of the loan. (Later on in this chapter, I'll show you how to negotiate more flexible terms with lenders.) Also, the lender generally will know if the fire insurance is current.

Negotiating for Profit

You've now determined that the true market value of the property is approximately $100,000. As an example, you thoroughly examine the house and decide that it needs approximately $2,000 of fix-up work to put it in good shape. Let's assume that you've determined the following amount owed on the property:

$60,000	1st deed trust
10,000	2nd deed of trust
2,500	Back payments and penalties
1,000	Back taxes
2,000	Projected fix-up
$75,500	

You know that you cannot pay more than eighty percent of the market value, or $80,000, for this piece of property and still ensure a good profit for yourself. The seller indicates to you that his rock-bottom offer is $85,000. You have two challenges:

1. How to acquire this nice house with little or none of your own money (I'll show you how in just a moment).

2. How to buy this house for $80,000 or below.

If time is running short—that is, the auction date is near—gently point out that if he doesn't do something by that date, the seller will lose everything. You then offer to take over all existing loans and purchase the house in "as is" condition for approximately $75,000. Point out that you could prepare a deed then and there.

Why would a seller consider this offer? Point out that if he loses the property to foreclosure, his credit will be blemished for seven years. He may not even be able to buy a car.

Another approach that I have found effective is known as the "what if . . ." approach. It works like this: Explain to Mr. Tardy that in the unlikely case that a miracle stumbled into his life and a real estate broker were to bring him a full-price offer tomorrow, a large number of costs might actually be charged to Mr. Tardy. For example:

$100,000	Purchase price
− 6,000	6% commission
− 3,000	3% closing costs: title, escrow, etc.
− 1,000	1% prepayment penalty (could be more)
− 3,000	FHA/VA loan points
− 2,000	Fix-up costs
$ 85,000	Actual net price to seller

$ 85,000	
−73,500	Loans, back payments, back taxes
$ 11,500	Amount seller would receive

Remember, the seller would receive this amount only if a major miracle took place. A last-minute buyer would have to swoop down from the heavens just in the nick of time to pay full market value for the property. This is the *best* the seller could do under ideal circumstances; and, of course, he realizes that he is well past the time to hope for ideal circumstances

On the other hand, you could guarantee that your offer is genuine and would be completed. He has little hope the other offer would be forthcoming.

Creative Offers and Formulas

I have found that approximately twenty-five percent of homeowners in the latter stages of foreclosure are willing to throw up their hands and rid themselves of their property for one dollar and a notarized signature on a deed. I've also discovered that the vast majority of people want something for their equity and will even risk a total loss at the auction block if they sense that you're being totally financially ruthless with them. Let's examine some ways in which both the empire builder and the distressed homeowner can benefit in this transaction. As an empire builder, you would like to buy the property using little or none of your own money at eighty percent of market value or less. The seller would like, and may even need, some money in order to move through the transaction comfortably.

Formula #89 Refinance for Equity
Offer the seller $3,000 cash for his equity in the property. You could then figure your acquisition costs as follows:

Purchase price	$76,500
Assume 1st deed of trust	$60,000
Assume 2nd deed of trust	10,000
Pay back payments	$ 2,500
Pay back taxes	1,000
Down payment for seller's equity	3,000
Cash out of pocket	$ 6,500

Let's assume that you don't have a lot of spare cash, but want to cash in on foreclosure opportunities. What can you do? Borrow approximately $8,500 on a short-term line of credit from any of the following sources:

1. Private friend, relative, business associate

2. Bank

3. Credit cards

4. Overdraft privileges

5. Credit union

6. Insurance policy

You would spend the $8,500 in the following manner:

$3,000	To acquire seller's equity
2,500	Pay back payments and costs
1,000	Pay back taxes
2,000	Fix up property
$8,500	Total loan spent

How would you pay this short-term line of credit back? Because the property is now in top condition, it may command a higher appraisal. But for our purposes, let's assume that the property is worth a solid $100,000. It would be relatively easy to refinance the property through a conventional lender for, let's say, eighty percent of the $100,000, or $80,000. The new $80,000 loan would pay off the following:

$60,000	1st deed of trust
10,000	2nd deed of trust
8,500	Short-term loan payback
1,500	New loan costs
$80,000	New 1st deed of trust

You've just bought a property out of foreclosure at eighty percent of the market value for nothing down.

Now let's see how we can do this and actually put cash in our pockets.

Formula #90   Foreclosure Crank
Very simply, you could get an eighty-five percent loan to the $100,000 value which would yield $85,000 to be disbursed as follows:

$60,000	1st deed of trust
10,000	2nd deed of trust
8,500	Short-term loan payback
1,500	New loan costs
5,000	Cash in your pocket
$85,000	

An eighty-five percent investor loan can currently be gotten through FHA, some conventional savings and loans, and through programs associated with Fannie Mae.

Formula #91   Second Note Discounts
Another method of buying the property for nothing down and putting cash in your pocket when only eighty percent loans to value are available involves discounting the second lender. Let's assume that we have a commitment from Avarice Savings and Loan for an $80,000 new first loan. We decide that we should receive compensation for our time invested in the project. We need cash to buy food and to pay our day-to-day bills. The only way to generate cash in your pocket is to discount any or all of the amounts to be paid off.

I have found that private second mortgage holders are the most receptive to a discount. Let's assume that we offer the second mortgage holder $7,000 to clear his $10,000 debt. Why would he accept a $3,000 discount on the amount owed? There are several possible reasons, including:

1. The $10,000 owed to him might be paid back over a five- or six-year period or longer. Most people recognize that they would rather have cash now than in five years.

There is a time value to money. Therefore, most people will trade a future promise to pay for a discounted amount of cash on hand.

2. The lender may need the money for other investments, college bills, vacations, home improvements, etc.

3. The lender probably feels a little unsettled, having recently gone through a foreclosure process. He may be very nervous about the security of the house and what might happen if he has to go through another foreclosure. Unless the lenders are professional investors, their primary objective is just to get paid. A secure discounted immediate payment might prove to be quite attractive. In that case, your $80,000 loan would work like this:

$60,000	1st trust deed
7,000	2nd trust deed (discounted)
8,500	Short-term loan
1,500	Loan costs
$77,000	Paid out
$ 3,000	Cash in your pocket

Formula #92   Subordination in Foreclosure

As an alternative to the above strategy, ask the secondary lender to subordinate his $10,000 second mortgage to a new first mortgage of $80,000. This means that the $10,000 second mortgage on the property would not be paid off by the new $80,000 loan; instead, it would remain as a $10,000 second deed of trust on the house.

New 1st deed of trust	$80,000	
Pay-off amounts	60,000	Old 1st
	8,500	Short-term loan
	1,500	Loan fees
Total paid out	70,000	
Cash in your pocket	$10,000	

You might notice that the loans on the property total more than you paid for it.

$80,000	1st deed of trust
10,000	2nd deed of trust
$90,000	Total loans against the property

However, you should still feel fairly safe, since the total loans on the property ($90,000) still equal only ninety percent of the market value ($100,000). The net result is that you bought a property at ninety percent of market value and put $10,000 cash in your pocket. We'll talk more about working with lenders during and after the foreclosure process toward the end of this chapter.

Formula #93   Refinance the Second

As an alternative to refinancing the first deed of trust, you could refinance the second to pay off the back payments and cover your other costs. Let's look at how the numbers would work for this one:

Assume	$60,000	1st deed of trust
New	20,000	2nd deed of trust
	$80,000	
Pay-offs	$10,000	Old 2nd deed of trust
	8,500	Short-term loan
	1,500	Loan costs
New 2nd	$20,000	

By getting a second mortgage loan for more than $20,000 you could even put cash in your pocket, or use the extra proceeds for fixing up the property.

Formula #94   Share the Profits

Because foreclosure profits can be so lucrative when a good transaction comes along, don't hesitate to use a partner. Many friends of mine who work full time making money in foreclosures have private parties available to them to front any cash necessary to take advantage of a super deal. In the transaction which we are discussing, the partner must come up with $8,500 cash. What benefits will the partner derive from such a deal? Typically, the partner will receive all his initial cash back upon the successful refinancing of the property, plus twenty-five to fifty percent ownership in the property.

One necessary caution to the creative empire builder is to make sure that you do all your homework. Foreclosures can be tricky. It would be good to work with a competent real estate attorney or experienced title officer on the first couple of transactions, particularly when you're risking somebody else's money.

Formula #95 Using Your Credit (the "Santa Clause")

One way in which the seller can win and remain in his home is for you to co-sign with him to get a new first loan for the $80,000. With that $80,000 you can pay off the old loans, bring current the back payments and taxes, and still have fix-up money available.

Are you truly the Santa Claus for whom this poor soul has been longing? Not really! As you make this gracious proposition to Mr. and Mrs. Tardy, they bubble with joy. When they are both ready to kneel before you and kiss your hand, you drop a bombshell. "I want something, too," you state.

The adoration stops, and Mr. and Mrs. Tardy jump to their feet with a "What?"

"I would like half ownership in your home in exchange for my co-signing on the loan." If the Tardies object to this, explain that you won't co-sign otherwise. Point out the following advantages to Mr. and Mrs. Tardy:

1. They do not get thrown out of their home.

2. They still own and have an investment in half a house.

3. Their kids do not change schools.

4. They do not suffer the humiliation of foreclosure.

5. They preserve their credit.

I would not make this offer to every foreclosure victim. Some people in foreclosure, unfortunately, are "deadbeats." The worst person you can have as a partner is a deadbeat.

You might choose to offer this alternative to someone who generally is hardworking and responsible, but who for various reasons may be having a difficult time making ends meet. The most important criterion I use when offering this alternative is that the economic situation is temporary. If you have good credit, this is an excellent way in which to enter the profitable foreclosure market without money and to avoid future management hassles.

Make your offer to the seller, and make every effort to get a signed acceptance that evening or day. Emphasize a sense of immediacy. If the seller is still reluctant to sign a purchase agreement on your proposal, leave the offer with him and indicate that unless you hear from him by the next day, you will be buying another piece of property.

In my experience, the best place to pick up a foreclosure is during the default period, working directly with the seller. You'll find sellers more flexible and less profit-oriented than bankers are after repossession (although you will find later in the chapter strategies for dealing with bankers). Also, if you wait and attempt to buy property at the auction block you will find a little more competition and generally a requirement for a heavy cash outlay.

AREA TWO: BUYING AT AUCTION

One of the most fascinating areas in which to profit with foreclosures is when the property is being sold at what is generally known as a trustee's sale. The foreclosure auction is probably one of the last bastions of true cutthroat capitalism in the U.S. today. Generally, the people you'll see at an auction are professionals who make their full-time living buying and selling foreclosures. As such, in many locales they often make behind-the-scenes deals with each other where each will be allowed to get a property but will not interfere in the bidding process—that is, they agree not to unnecessarily bid up the prices of the property for each other. This is illegal in every state that I know of, so if someone offers you any favors or money to keep the auction bidding noncompetitive, be aware that you're being asked to participate in a crime.

The beneficiary of the loan which is being foreclosed appoints a trustee or auctioneer to sell the property in a public place. The trustee or auctioneer might initiate the auction in this manner: "On behalf of the beneficiary, Hapless Savings and Loan, I am authorized to bid $60,000." Next, the trustee might further suggest that he'll accept bids in specific increments, such as $500 or $1,000.

At a foreclosure sale, cash or a cashier's check is generally required to buy the property. This fact limits your competition considerably. However, where the competition is limited, your potential for profit is great. How can you cash in on the tremendous profits at foreclosure auctions, where properties routinely sell for fifty percent and sixty percent of the true market value, even if you have little or no cash?

Formula #96   Line Up Financing in Advance

After thorough investigation of the property, go to a mortgage lender well before the bidding date. Explain to the lender the details of the property and the maximum amount you will be bidding on the property. The lender will, of course, need an application and an appraisal on the property to verify the facts.

If the amount you request falls within the lender's loan-to-value ratio (this figure varies with each lender and each property, but a good guideline would be seventy percent to eighty percent of the appraised value), then he might commit to lend you the funds for the property after you take title.

In exchange for the letter of commitment, the lender might charge a one percent commitment fee. This one percent refers to one percent of the total loan commitment. For example, if you needed a commitment for $60,000 the fee would be $600. If you're an unsuccessful bidder, the lender could keep that $600.

Take the letter of commitment to your bank and use it as security to get a short-term $60,000 loan in the form of a cashier's check. By using this strategy, you can buy properties at foreclosure sales for nothing down.

AREA THREE: MOTIVATED LENDERS

The property has been sold at auction and it appears that you've missed a golden opportunity; but wait, the property has been sold back to the lender because nobody offered more than the minimum bid. You can still purchase this property and make a profit, although you will have to use a low-key approach.

Generally, lenders such as banks, savings and loans, and finance companies are not in the business of owning real property. They're in business to lend money. In fact, the law sets a limit on the amount of real estate a bank or savings and loan can own. Also, the lenders' own boards of directors get very uncomfortable if they have many foreclosed properties on their balance sheets. It displays for all to see the bad loans a financial institution has made. The last thing a banker wants is to advertise to its depositors the fact that bad loans are made. In order to hide these foreclosed properties, bankers place them as a footnote in the annual deposit balance sheet under the label R.E.O. R.E.O. stands for Real Estate Owned.

During the last several years many banks, savings and loans, and finance companies have had to foreclose on an unusually high number of properties. They've become the ultimate motivated seller. I talked to a banker in the Detroit area recently who indicated that he had over 200 R.E.O.s on his books, and that he would sell most of them for nothing down.

Approaching the Banker

Don't expect to waltz up to a desperate banker and have him immediately whip out his list of R.E.O.s at your first inquiry. My first experience in approaching a banker went something like this:

"Could I see your list of R.E.O.s?" I asked.

The banker looked at me dumbfounded, cleared his throat, frowned, and said, "We really don't have many of those in this bank, young man."

I walked away, figuring that either the instructions I

had gotten at a recent seminar I had attended were wrong, or I had chosen the wrong bank.

I found out later, as I established a more solid relationship with this particular banker, that he actually did have several R.E.O. properties available. But again, banks don't want to advertise information like that, and they usually won't admit it to every stranger who strolls in off the street. Generally, to get that list of R.E.O. properties, the following hints have helped me overcome bankers' reluctance to divulge this information:

1. Try to establish a good banking relationship with the loan officer at the bank. (In some cases, large banks will have property offices with certain people in charge of R.E.O.s. Establish a line of credit, and stop by and let the loan officer know what you're doing. Let him know your success.

2. If that takes too long for your program, find somebody you know to introduce you to a successful investor. Bankers will very rarely give out R.E.O. information to someone they don't know, but they become more cooperative when they think that you have the ability to help them.

3. Be persistent when asking for that list of R.E.O. properties. When the banker denies such a list exists, tactfully ask, "Who should I see in the bank to find out about some of the problem properties you own?"

Formula #97   R.E.O.s

Some lenders are so motivated that they are wiling to sell R.E.O property for practically nothing down. In actuality, most banks and savings and loans do not like to have loans on their books for which there were no down payments. There are state laws that limit the amount of this type of loan that can be made by certain financial institutions.

Any loan with a very low down payment must be called a "loan to facilitate" when bank examiners audit these banks. Auditors can be very critical of these types of loans. Therefore, Mr. Banker must be very careful if he wants to solve his R.E.O. problems.

Mr. Banker might be willing to lend you, on a short-term line of credit, a down payment which must be equal to twenty percent of the selling price. For example, let's say the bank will sell the R.E.O. for $60,000. You figure that in its present condition the property is worth at least $75,000. The bank will loan you on a short-term line of credit $12,000, or twenty percent of the $60,000 selling price. The bank then will give you a mortgage for $48,000, or eighty percent of the selling price. This ploy gives the bank two legitimate loans on its books and you a nice piece of property for nothing down.

Formula #98   Fix-up Work

The bank can even loan you more than the selling price of the property if the added loan amount is to be used for fixing up the property. The lender may want to impound part of the money and disburse funds only upon completion of the work.

How do you pay this short-term credit line back? When the work is finished, the property should be more valuable. The bank would probably commit to refinance the property at eighty percent of the new appraisal value. For example, if the new property appraisal was $80,000, the lender could safety loan eighty percent of $80,000, which is $64,000.

$64,000		New 1st loan	
	$48,000	Old 1st loan	⎛ Payoff ⎞
	12,000	Short-term loan	⎝ Amounts ⎠
	4,000	Fix-up loan	
	$64,000		

ADVANTAGES TO LENDER

1. Get the black mark of an R.E.O. off the books.

2. Convert a dead problem asset to a good loan and cash flow.

3. Get a higher interest rate.

4. Loan officer is the hero.

Formula #99   The Lender Can Help

Besides making price and down payment concessions, motivated lenders can be flexible with all the basic financial terms surrounding a transaction. You can assume the first mortgage and ask the second lender to advance the back payments necessary to bring the first current, and perhaps even ask the second lender to waive the back interest.

The first lender might be amenable to an assumption without a higher interest rate because it is a foreclosure property that the lender does not want to own.

The secondary lender may not have a large equity cushion, so therefore does not want to take title to the house. For example, if the first loan was $60,000 and the second was $30,000 and it was estimated that market value for the property was only $95,000, the secondary lender could end up losing money if his foreclosure costs, rehabilitation, and cost for making up back payments exceeded $5,000. To avoid such a loss a secondary or first lender might be willing to advance back payments and forgive back interest.

Variations

Variations to the previous formula include any of the following strategies:

1. Moratorium period on payments on the first or any junior loan.

2. Lower the interest on the note.

3. Adjust the principal amount on the note.

Formula #100   More Subordination

You could have the secondary lender subordinate his position on the property so that you could put a new second on it. The proceeds you would receive from the

new second mortgage could be used to pay back payments
and bills and to rehabilitate the property. It would work
like this:

$60,000	1st deed of trust
10,000	New 2nd deed of trust to pay off back bills
15,000	3rd deed of trust (former 2nd deed of trust)
$85,000	

A variation of this technique might allow the seller or,
lo and behold, the buyer to pocket cash. Let's assume that
instead of the $10,000 new second mortgage being entirely
used to pay off back bills, payments, and rehabilitation
costs, that only $5,000 was necessary to cover these fees.
This would leave $5,000 to pay the seller or yourself $5,000.
This is another nothing down foreclosure technique you
can get started on tomorrow.

Private Lenders

You'll find that many of the private lenders who own
second and third mortgages on properties are simply former owners who sold their properties but weren't able to
get all cash at the time of sale due to unfavorable market
conditions. Most of these people don't want their own
property back and generally don't understand or want the
hassle associated with a foreclosure.

You can use this particular insight when you deal with
private party secondary lenders. Show a private lender a
way to protect his note with a reasonable schedule for
salvaging some or all of his note amount and you'll find a
very flexible person with whom to deal.

Formula #101   *Substitution of Collateral*

Let's assume that a private lender is the beneficiary on a
second deed of trust on a property going into foreclosure.
You feel that this property offers an opportunity for a
quick profit. The numbers might work like this:

$50,000	1st deed of trust
10,000	2nd deed of trust
2,500	Back payments on second
$62,500	Total amount owed

You have an appraisal done on the property and it comes out at $75,000. You know that you can resell it to an investor friend almost immediately at $68,000, or about ten percent under market. Let's look at your potential profit if you did this.

$50,000	1st
10,000	2nd
2,500	Costs
$62,500	
$68,000	Sale price
62,500	Buying price and costs
$ 5,500	Your profit

Is $5,500 really your profit? Haven't we forgotten that the seller in foreclosure may want some money before deeding you the house? Let's say that the seller needs $2,500 cash as incentive to sell his house. When we deduct $2,500 from our $5,500 gross profit in the transaction ($5,500 − 2,500 = $3,000), it leaves us with only about $3,000 net profit for our time and effort.

That amount of money may be worthwhile to you, depending on your time and capital input into the transaction. But let's say that a $3,000 net profit on the transaction would not be acceptable to you. You want more! (That's the fundamental cause for all growth in life.) Here's how you can generate more cash from this transaction.

Ask the beneficiary of the second deed of trust if he would take another piece of property of yours as security for the note he owns. Moreover, we are offering to substitute collateral for the note he owns.

You show the beneficiary that he could have safer security than he has on a property with a pending foreclosure. You could show the seller your credit report, and an appraisal that gives the beneficiary assurance that there's adequate security in your other property.

Why would you want to do this? You would be freeing up saleable equity, for which you would get the cash promptly. It would work like this:

Property #1
(In foreclosure)
Sales price $68,000
Total liens $62,500

$50,000	First trust deed
(10,000)	Second trust deed
(2,500)	Costs
$50,000	Total liens

Property #2
(Investor's secure house)
Market value $75,000
Total liens $40,000

$40,000	First trust deed
12,500	New second trust deed
$52,500	Total liens

You will also notice that we move the back payments into the new second loan on my house. How does this complicated maneuver help me? I can sell the property to my investor friend for $68,000, and now I only owe $50,000, the amount of the first note, on that particular property.

$68,000	Selling price
50,000	1st loan assumed by investor
$18,000	Cash I get from the transaction

This is not total profit. In effect, my profit is still only $3,000. However, I was able to borrow against another asset of mine simultaneously with this transaction. The real advantage I gain is generating more cash versus my time input on one transaction.

Secondly, if the beneficiary is willing to take raw land or

another marginally lendable asset as security, you've in effect gotten a loan on a generally unleveragable asset. It's almost impossible to get second loans on raw land. If you could move an existing note that is facing a foreclosure problem to your raw land and then generate cash from the freed-up equity left by moving the note, you're operating in the big leagues. You are functioning as a successful professional creative real estate investor. In fact, only a small percentage of the professionals ever use ideas like these.

The purpose of sharing creative ideas of this nature with you is two-fold. In the first place, I want to show you a possible solution to an investment problem you might face. Secondly, and more importantly, I want to shape your attitude that once we learn the basic rules of the real estate game, the spectrum of ways in which we can solve problems and thus make a fortune is only limited by our dreams, visions, and goals.

CHAPTER 17
Equity Sharing: The New Wave

Headlines from magazines and newspapers in recent years have pounded on the question, "Is home ownership dead?" In a country where almost sixty percent of the adult population owns a home, will that trend continue? Will fluctuating interest rates and high building costs prevent most young Americans from ever being able to own a home of their own?

What does it all mean? It's been estimated that less than twelve percent of the adult population can afford to buy an average priced house using conventional mortgages. Does this portend the end of home ownership as we know it?

I don't think so! Innovation is the pulse of our nation. To cope with high down payments, fluctuating interest rates, and tight income restrictions, an important type of financial arrangement is being used, and that arrangement is known as equity sharing.

Equity sharing is not a new way to finance real estate transactions. Professional investors have been pooling funds in partnerships and syndications for years to acquire apartment buildings, commercial structures, farms, etc. However, it is only recently that people have begun to apply this technique to the single family house.

HOMEBUYER AND INVESTOR PROBLEMS

When inflation exceeded the rate of interest banks charged on home mortgage loans in the late seventies and early eighties, it became obvious that dramatic changes were due in our financial system. These changes took the form of higher interest rates, shorter loan terms, and an aggressive attack on the assumability of old low-interest-rate loans.

These changes, along with already high house prices, created enormous obstacles for the would-be first-time homebuyer. Because of strict guidelines followed by most conventional lenders, a twenty percent down payment is generally required for them to consider a loan. On an $80,000 house, this amounts to $16,000. Have you tried to save $16,000 cash today? It could take even the most disciplined young couple years to save that amount of money.

At this stage of the book, you know that purchasing

property with a loan from a conventional lender is only one of hundreds of ways of financing property. However, the average Joe Lunchbucket is intimidated by the awesome requirements today's banks and savings and loans have. For those who haven't unlocked their creative energies, or for those who want things done simply, equity sharing is the answer.

Formula #102   Equity Sharing Solutions

If you can't come up with a down payment of $16,000, for example, simply bring in a partner. Most young people buying houses today do this on a more informal basis than I'm suggesting. They borrow from parents, relatives, or friends for that first down payment.

What if you don't have rich relatives? Are you out of luck? Remember, the empire builder's motto is, "That which we don't have, we can get." Bring an investor into the transaction to put up the down payment, with you, the buyer, handling the monthly payment, bank interest, taxes, and other expenses.

Your investor-partner would get all his down payment cash back first when a sale occurs, and each of you would split the new growth in equity fifty-fifty. You will need to determine how long your agreement will run. I generally suggest that equity sharing agreements should last at least five years. Any shorter period than that leads to false expectations as to how quickly each party thinks the property will appreciate. Five years tends to affirm in each co-owner's mind that real estate is a long-term investment.

I find it best to have the occupants or co-tenants of the house handle all repairs up to $75 per month. Any amount in excess of $75 per month can be classified as a capital improvement, and as such should be split equally between the owning partners. Although again, I must point out, everything is negotiable.

Security

What if Mr. and Mrs. Moneybags put up a down payment for you and you don't make the payments? What recourse do the poor Moneybags have?

They could have you sign a note secured by a specific part of the property. If you didn't make the payments, the Moneybags could foreclose on your half of the property. If you are still in possession after the foreclosure, they could have you evicted, as should be spelled out in your agreement. Have a competent real estate attorney draft a good equity sharing agreement. (If you would like a good format and want to save a significant portion of your legal fees, I have a set of proven equity share agreements which you can order from the back of this book.)

Variations

1. If you have part of a down payment, bring an investor in to pay the balance and split the ownership and profits accordingly.

2. If you have the down payment but can't come up with the monthly payment, bring an investor in to help subsidize that monthly amount. Give the investor a piece of the action in proportion to his contribution. For example, if you put up $16,000 cash and your investor subsidizes a monthly payment of $300 per month for five years, or sixty months, that would equal $18,000. I would say that you should receive approximately sixty percent of the profits after each of you receive your initial cash back. The investor would receive approximately forty percent of the profits.

Are you puzzled? After all, the investor put up $18,000 and you put up $16,000. The difference here is that the investor put up his $18,000 over a five-year period. You put your money up immediately. I would discount the investor's money to between $12,000 and $13,000 in present value.

Also, you found the investment, lived in the house, and

cared for it all those years. This subjective value entitles you to a little larger chunk of the equity.

3. At times, to attract investors it's good to add some enticements. At a seminar I was teaching in Orlando, one of my students shared this variation with me. He had been approached by a young fellow who asked my student if he would be interested in putting up the down payment on the young fellow's house.

The student knew this young guy, and was impressed with his ambition and responsibility, so here is how the offer went. "You put up $10,000 for the down payment on my house, and you'll earn money in two ways. Number one, I'll split the profits with you equally when we sell the house. Secondly, when we sell, you'll get your cash back first, plus an eighteen percent return on that money you invested."

Do I recommend that you offer an eighteen percent return of investor down payment money plus a fifty percent ownership in the property? Certainly not! The young fellow offered too much. The rate of return on real estate investments will beat any other means of making money even with three percent or four percent appreciation rates. An incentive of half ownership is completely adequate. Perhaps, and this is only in desperate circumstances (and you should never be desperate if you plan properly), you might add an interest incentive of seven or eight percent. However, if you are the investor someone offers this eighteen percent return to, you've probably just been given a no-lose bonanza, if the property and the buyer check out.

Formula #103   Lease-Option, Equity Sharing Variation

Try leasing back with an option to purchase your prospective home. In this instance, Mr. and Mrs. Moneybags actually buy the property using their cash and financial statement. You agree to lease it back for the amount of the Moneybags' monthly payment; however, you want an option to purchase fifty percent of the property at any time in the next five years.

If structured properly, Mr. and Mrs. Moneybags get the

tax benefits the rental property offers, as well as some good possibilities for fifty percent of the appreciation. You get a nice home in which to live and some nice potential appreciation benefits.

Formula #104   Equity Sharing Option

Give Mr. and Mrs. Moneybags an option to purchase fifty percent or more of your prospective home for one dollar. In exchange, have them provide the cash down payment.

They control a trouble-free appreciating investment; you get a nice home and fifty percent of the appreciation benefits. This is clearly a situation where both parties win.

Let's look at other variables that are negotiable in an equity sharing plan:

- Cash down payment: split, his, yours, friend

- Monthly payments (expenses): split, his, yours, friend

- Time period of agreement

- Maintenance split over a specific amount, e.g., $25

- What happens when time period is up?

- Buy-out agreement or trade-out agreement

- How is equity appreciation shared?

- Option or ownership

- Tax benefits

- Default clauses

WHY EQUITY SHARING SUITS INVESTORS

Generally, we assume that the major problem for a would-be empire builder is the lack of money. However, a problem that is just as vexing to other empire builders is how to maximize the yield on the cash they have available.

There's an old axiom, "That which you don't use, you lose." All investors are looking to find the highest return on their money with total safety and the least amount of

Formula #103: Lease-Option, Equity Sharing Vacation

REAL ESTATE PURCHASE AGREEMENT
AND RECEIPT FOR DEPOSIT

This is intended to be a legally binding contract. Read it carefully.

_____ , _____ , _____ , 19 ___
        (City)   (State)

Received from _____ ,
                 (Name)

herein called Buyer, the sum of _____

_____ dollars $ _____ , in the form of cash ☐ ,

cashier's check ☐ personal check ☐ or _____ ☐ payable to
            (Name)
_____ , to be held uncashed

until acceptance of this offer, as deposit on account of purchase price of _____

_____ dollars $ _____

for the purchase of property located in _____ ,
                (City)

County of _____ , _____ .
   (County)   (State)

described as follows: _____
        (Address or other legal description)

Buyer will deposit in escrow with _____
        (Title company or other third party)

the balance of purchase price as follows: _____

    1.   This is a lease-option agreement with the following terms
        and conditions:

       a)   The buyer agrees to lease this property for 5 years
           with the option to purchase 50% interest of ownership
           by paying option fee of $9,000.

       b)   The buyer agrees to take care of all maintenance on
           the property during lease period.

       c)   The buyer will pay $600 per month lease payments for
           5 years, of which $150 per month will be credited
           toward option fees.

       d)   This agreement is to be recorded.

Detail above any factual terms and conditions applicable to this sale, such as financing, contingency of sale of other property, the disposition of structural pest control inspection, and repairs and personal property to be included in the sale.

Deposit will ☐ will not ☐ be increased by $ _____ to $ _____
within _____ days of acceptance of this offer.

Buyer does ☐ does not ☐ intend to occupy subject property as his residence.

The supplements initialed below are incorporated as part of this agreement.

____ Structural Pest Control Certification Agreement   ____ VA Amendment
____ Special Studies Zone Disclosure   ____ FHA Amendment
____ Flood Insurance Disclosure   ____ Other _____
____ Occupancy Agreement   ____ Other _____

Buyer and Seller acknowledge receipt of a copy of this page, which constitutes page 1 of _____ Pages.

X _____   X _____
  Buyer   Seller

X _____   X _____
  Buyer   Seller

effort on their part. Equity sharing in single family homes, if properly structured, is in my opinion one such ideal investment vehicle. Let's look at the advantages to the investor.

1. Virtually no management is necessary. The co-tenant or occupant of the property is part owner and therefore has a vested interest in maintaining its condition and increasing its value.

2. Negative cash flow is eliminated. If the investor puts up the money and the co-tenants handle the P.I.T.I. (principal, interest, taxes, and insurance) and minor repairs, it eliminates the need for a monthly investor contribution of money.

3. If structured properly, the investor might be able to get as much as fifty percent of all tax benefits.

4. Equity sharing eliminates geographic restrictions. Because management is eliminated, you could successfully own properties throughout the United States.

5. Using any of the no down payment formulas, you could buy a house for nothing down, equity share it, and have no negative cash flow and no management. With a system like this, you could pyramid yourself to financial independence in just a few short years. Here's how it works.

Formula #105   Ideal Investment System

Let's say that you've just found a motivated seller who needs some cash, but he indicates that he will be very flexible with the terms. You remember reading about the "wedge and cap" technique in Chapter 9 of my book and decide to structure an offer based on that idea. The seller wants $60,000 and currently owes $30,000 on an FHA first mortgage at nine percent interest, payable at $310 per month P.I.T.I.

$60,000	Asking price
30,000	1st mortgage
$30,000	Equity

The seller, of course, would like all cash for his equity. However, since his house has been on the market for a long time, a heavy dose of realism has had an effect on him. Mr. Motivation knows and accepts that some of his equity will have to be taken back in the form of a note and paid off in the future.

He does need at least $10,000 cash, with which he will buy another house, so here's your offer:

$30,000	1st mortgage (you assume)
10,000	New 2nd mortgage
20,000	3rd mortgage carried by seller
$60,000	

You offer the seller full price. Why? Because you are asking for very flexible terms on the transaction. You can assume the first mortgage, since it is an FHA loan which is fully assumable at the same low rate of interest and payment schedule.

You ask the seller to put a new second mortgage on the property so he can generate the needed $10,000 cash. Make sure that this second mortgage is assumable. If Mr. Motivation can't or won't put the second mortgage on the property, then you might have to accomplish this part of the transaction. It's important to understand that you will assume this debt of $10,000, and thus it becomes your financial obligation when you take title to the property.

Finally, we ask the seller to carry back the balance of his equity in the form of a note secured by a third deed of trust or mortgage, with the following terms: ten percent interest, no monthly payments for the first three years, and the interest is to accrue with simple interest, *not compound interest*. After three years, payments on the note start, amortized to retire the debt with equal monthly payments over a ten-year period. (There are many variations on this financing formula. Be creative and come up with five different terms for this note.)

We have structured a moratorium on the third mortgage which will keep our monthly payments low in the first few years. Let's look at the current monthly payment schedule.

$30,000	1st mortgage	$310/month
10,000	2nd mortgage	180/month
20,000	3rd mortgage	
$60,000		$490/month total
		payments for 2 years

Let's assume that if we rented this property, we could get $390 per month maximum—that leaves us with $490 − 390 = $100 negative cash flow. We can't afford this. We place the following ad in the newspaper:

Nothing Down
Nice 3 bedroom, 2 bath house.
Quiet neighborhood, payments
under $500 per month.
Call today   791-3000

Your phone will ring off the hook when people call on this ad. Explain to them that you will sell half ownership in this house to them for nothing down (although I generally get some type of security deposit), and that their payments for the first two years will only be $490 per month. Don't forget to tell them their payments will rise to approximately $690 after that time is up.

You will get lots of "takers" for a deal like this one. In effect, you own fifty percent of a house for nothing down, with no negative cash flow, no management or repair hassle, and most importantly, you can continue to find and buy deals like this one. There's no limit to the amount of property you could acquire in this manner. Frank A., one of my seminar graduates, bought over seventy-five houses last year using this technique. Bonnie W., in Orlando, Florida, another seminar graduate, has acquired over three million dollars' worth of houses in the last eighteen months. Because she bought these houses at a good price, her net worth is already in excess of one million dollars. She did this in an eighteen-month period starting without money. All she had was knowledge and a burning desire to succeed.

Formula #106   Never Sell

Suppose that you've been transferred to another city by your employer. You figure that you will have to sell the home in which you have been living in order to purchase a new residence.

Recently, you read a statistic indicating that homes in the United States had averaged annual price increases of almost thirteen percent. After thinking about that statistic for a moment, you realized that most of your own wealth is tied up in your home, and that if you had held on to your last house when a job transfer had occurred, how much better off financially you would be!

"Oh, well," you sigh, "I sure wish that we could keep this house and buy another too. But I guess we just don't have the money." That's nonsense. Again, ideas and solutions abound. Here is what you might consider doing. Refinance your existing home to generate the necessary cash to buy that new home in the city you're moving to.

"But what about those new higher payments?" you squeal. "If I rented out the old house, the rent wouldn't nearly cover that new higher payment. I would have a negative cash flow, and I just couldn't afford that."

Equity sharing might just be your answer. Here's how it might work: Let's say that you value your house at $60,000, and you owe $30,000 on it. When you refinance a property like this, you can generally get eighty percent of the value as a new loan. Therefore, you could probably get eighty percent of $60,000, or $48,000, on a new first mortgage. After paying off the old loan of $30,000, that would leave you with $18,000 cash. You could use this money as a down payment to buy your new home.

However, we still have the monthly payment problem. Advertise to equity share it. Sell fifty percent ownership in your old home for little or nothing down. In exchange, the co-tenant or occupant would make the monthly payment.

In order for this to work, the new loan placed on the property must be assumable. The co-tenant would give you a note secured by the property in the amount of $12,000. This note could be interest-free. This note protects you if the co-tenant defaults, and also allows you to get paid first when the property is finally sold. All future profits would be split fifty-fifty. This technique allows someone to buy a house even if they don't have a lot of money, and at the same time allows you to hold on to another one of those magnificent wealth building vehicles, the single family home.

Formula #107   Variations

1. A variation on the above example might provide you with more cash. Have the buyer (co-tenant) assume your new first mortgage and shop around for a new second mortgage for approximately ten percent of the house's value, or $6,000, and give you the cash. Your co-tenant will then make the payments on the $6,000 second mortgage in addition to paying on the $48,000 first mortgage that you already had on the property. The co-tenant would also give you a note secured by a third mortgage on the property, with no interest, for the balance of your equity.

Since you received the cash your co-tenant borrowed on the second mortgage, while he has had his payments increased by the amount he has to pay on the second, you will probably have to make some concessions in favor of your co-tenant when the house is finally sold.

You could agree to repay your co-tenant for the money he has paid out on the second mortgage before you divide the sale proceeds. After all the mortgages are taken care of, including your own third, you would deduct whatever the co-tenant has paid on the second from the profits and hand that amount over to him before the two of you split what remains. His payments on the second mortgage could increase his share of the proceeds to the point where you might only get one-third of the profits when the property is sold, but one-third share is still better than no share.

2. The co-tenant could even bring in another equity share partner to put up the additional $6,000. This idea would allow your co-tenant to bypass conventional lenders and the additional payments and costs involved in taking out a conventional loan.

3. *Another idea for you to generate additional cash is to take back an interest-bearing second and also a third mortgage for the balance of your equity.* After escrow closes, sell the second mortgage to an investor. There are investors, as discussed earlier, who buy notes secured by real property at a discount.

Formula #108 Builders' Solutions

Many builders are stuck with unsold inventory during real estate recessions. During high interest periods houses just don't sell unless builders get very imaginative. A few years ago, when interest rates were high, builders brought down the interest rate for the first few years of a loan. They used some of the proceeds from the sale of a property to pay the lender an amount that lowered the buyer's interest rate for the first few years of the loan. This ploy lowers monthly payment requirements for the buyer and moves inventory for the builder. The builder is willing to take a significantly reduced profit, and maybe no profit, just to stay in business until times get better.

I think a better strategy for builders would be to equity share their unsold inventory. Simply have the co-tenant take out a new permanent loan, replacing the builder's high-interest-rate construction loan, thereby relieving the builder of that burden. The builder could then take back a second mortgage interest-free for the balance of his equity.

The permanent loan placed on the property would probably exceed the construction loan. This would give the builder an immediate cash profit and still allow him the opportunity to get fifty percent of all future profits on the house through appreciation.

INNOVATIONS OF THE '80s

It seems that when an obstacle arises in any economic environment, innovative and energetic people rise to the challenge. With high interest rates, high prices, and high down payments, many young people saw home ownership as a vague and diminishing hope. Investors were hesitant to commit funds to properties with negative cash flows and management headaches in the real estate environment of the eighties.

In my opinion, equity sharing is the innovation that can allow home ownership to become a definite possibility in America once more. For investors, it offers extraordinary returns on invested dollars without the hassle of the traditional type of rental unit.

Does the success of equity sharing depend on inflation continuing? Not entirely. The average single family home has still been increasing in price by about five percent per year in the mid-'80s. And that was at a time when inflation was lower than it has been for quite some time. Even with this low five percent growth rate, the price of an average $80,000 house would increase to over $102,000 in just five years. And that's in a time of low inflation! What happens if the high rates of inflation return, as I think they will?

Other factors are influencing the upward price pressures on housing in this country. Demand is growing for housing as we see existing supplies dry up. The law of supply and demand, along with moderate increases in the inflation rate, will push prices to record levels in the next three or four years. Now is the last great buying opportunity for the next ten years. Equity sharing is one of the best innovative wealth building vehicles. In fact, *The Wall Street Journal*, in an article about equity sharing, says, "It's a concept that's here to stay."

CHAPTER 18
Structuring Notes to Maximize Profits

In today's uncertain economic climate, it is vital that you build maximum flexibility into the financing of each of your real estate transactions.

You build flexibility into transactions by creatively designing terms and provisions into the notes, deeds of trust, and mortgages that you sign. Most investors treat the note and deed of trust that they sign as a given, cast in cement. After all, these are standard documents that both parties automatically accept with only a casual discussion regarding terms and provisions.

Bankers, title companies, and attorneys readily supply us with these standard forms. In most cases, it is not in your best interest to sign these standard forms without careful consideration and scrutiny. Standard loan documents are designed for the average deal, and in most instances they favor the lender's interest.

You are not going to build a real estate empire very quickly by becoming involved in average deals. The empire builder needs to find and engineer exceptional deals. Each facet of any real estate deal represents present and future dollar profits. I want to show you how to turn the average deal into big profits by creatively engineering the terms and provisions of the lending documents.

THE SELLER IS MR. FLEXIBLE

When Mr. Banker loans us money to buy property, how flexible is he? Not very! Mr. Banker has designed lending documents to maximize his own monetary self interest. This type of loan might be considered hard. It can be expensive and adverse to our ability to maximize real estate profits. Mr. Banker is hard to deal with!

When Mr. Seller is involved in the financing of his property, can he be flexible with the terms and provisions? There is a very good chance that he will be quite flexible. We might call this loan "soft." Mr. Seller is a softy.

Why would Mr. Seller be such a softy about carrying back flexible terms and provisions on the financing? He has an additional motive that Mr. Banker does not have. Mr. Seller would like to sell his property. In today's market, motivated sellers are keenly aware that if they do not carry back some seller-financing at reasonable rates, they will have a much harder time selling their property.

Use Mr. Seller's primary motivation to create maximum flexibility in the notes you sign. An empire builder creates notes that solve present and future problems. Structure flexibility at the beginning of a transaction.

Let's look at some of the financing problems you will face in today's real estate market.

Negative Cash Flow

Negative cash flow, "eaters," or "alligators" all refer to the same problem in real estate: properties in which the owner must take money out of his pocket each month to service the monthly payment, taxes, insurance, and maintenance.

For example, I have a nice duplex that has monthly payments of $470 per month, P.I.T.I. (this refers to principal, interest, taxes, and insurance). The rent that I collect each month is $420. That means that I have a negative cash flow of approximately $50 per month ($470 – $420 = $50).

Why would I take on an "alligator" of this type? I'm betting that the value of the property will increase faster than $50 per month or $600 annual expenditure. In fact, this particular property should appreciate at least $6,000 in the next year, according to my projections. This is based on a ten percent appreciation rate.

This is a form of *creative debt*; you spend money on a monthly basis so that you can control an appreciating real estate asset. I'm betting on continued price appreciation in well-selected real estate.

The real estate empire builder's game is to control as much well-selected property as possible, as quickly as possible, then let inflation and your own creative application of improvements to the property do their work. For example, let's say that you buy $1,000,000 worth of good rental houses this year and just hold on by your fingernails, if necessary; in seven years, given a ten percent appreciation factor, you will have a net worth of approximately $1,000,000. It's the easy way to become a million-aire . . . but not so fast! In today's market, many properties are alligators. They eat away monthly at your money pouch. I know people who have acquired $1,000,000 worth of property indiscriminately, without properly designing their financing. They have negative cash flows of $2,000 to $3,000 each month. Unless you have a high cash flow, taking on big alligators can be economic suicide. If you don't have a short-term way of reducing the alligator's appetite, you are jeopardizing your entire real estate empire building program.

Don't fret! Solutions abound to the negative cash flow problem. I'm going to show you how to deal with that alligator, put him on a diet, and I'll show you how to hold on to your real estate empire comfortably even in hard times.

Solution #1   *Larger Cash Down Payment*

The traditional way in which investors control negative cash flows is to put a larger cash down payment into the transaction. This technique is especially relevant in times of high interest rates. With a larger down payment, you can assume older loans with lower interest rates. This can keep payments significantly lower than having to get a new loan at five or six percentage points higher than the assumable older loan on the property.

Normally, I wouldn't recommend this method. You won't get maximum leverage, and you will run out of cash pretty quickly. However, if you have a lot of cash and want to play it conservatively in these economic times, this is a great way of getting excellent consistent and safe returns on investment dollars.

Using the no down payment philosophy, you might consider bringing in a partner for the large cash outlay. You gain the dual advantage of using the low-interest assumable loan without a heavy cash outlay.

Solution #2   *Interest Only*

Structure the seller carryback note to have payments of interest only, with a balloon payment at a future date.

This lowers the monthly payment from a regular amortized loan. Let's look at an example:

Mr. Seller would like to carry back a $20,000 note at twelve percent interest, amortized over a ten-year period, payable at $286.95 per month. You might be better off offering a twelve percent interest-only loan, payable at $200 per month. You would eliminate a monthly "eat" of $86.95 per month. Multiply that times ten houses, and you get $869.50 per month saved. You could arrange to have Mr. Seller receive a balloon payment for the principal balance at the end of, let's say, six years, or any mutually agreeable time period.

What do you do when a balloon payment comes due? The property should be worth a lot more money. Let's look at some of your alternatives:

- You could refinance institutionally, i.e., bank, savings and loan

- Borrow from a loan broker, finance company, credit union

- Borrow from friend, family, acquaintance

- Request an extension for higher interest

- Renegotiate the loan

- Find a partner

- Make the note holder a partner (shared appreciation)

- Trade note holder out of the note

- Sell property

You see, there are no lack of alternatives. Don't let the sound of a big balloon six years down the line worry you. On the other hand, try not to get involved in one- or two-year balloon notes. Make them longer. Any mistakes you make generally get covered by inflation over time.

Solution #3   The "Backdoor"
In the balloon payment notes that you sign, it is wise to provide a "backdoor" clause. The backdoor clause pro-

vides a comfortable alternative to having to come up with all the cash to make that balloon payment. You need this clause in case the money market has gone crazy, which might make refinancing difficult or impossible. You will be at a distinct disadvantage trying to renegotiate the note at balloon payment time if alternatives are not spelled out ahead of time.

Negotiate a backdoor clause into all your transactions including balloon payments. Let us look at some possible ingredients in backdoor clauses:

- Convert loan balance to an amortized loan

- Provide for a six-month or nine-month extension in case the prime rate is not at some mutually agreeable point

- If you can't find the money, let the seller conduct a search for funds.

- Convert the lender to a partner

- Convert the loan balance to a high-payment amortized loan, e.g., $1,000 per month until paid . . . yuck!

- Pay off part of the loan

- Share appreciation with the lien holder

- Pay a bonus for an extension

Solution #4   Seasonal Flows

Design the note payments to meet the seasonal demands of the property.

There is a college town in Northern California called Chico. During the school year, it is difficult to find a vacancy in the entire town. During the summer, when many of the students go home, empty apartments and houses are in abundance. Whenever I write an offer on rental property in this town, I try to structure the owner carryback financing in the following manner: Let's say that the owner is expecting $200 per month on a carryback note. "I would be willing to do that," I say, "but I would like to have a moratorium on payments for two months of the summer." *If Mr. Seller accepts, I have effectively shifted all the vacancy risk to him.*

If he doesn't go for that idea, try to get him to reduce the payment during the summer. He then shares the vacancy risk.

Solution #5 Going with the Flow

A variation on this last technique might be called a performance trust deed. Let's say that you are willing to buy an apartment building. The only problem is that Mr. Seller doesn't have any proof of his income and expenses.

To bring a higher degree of certainty into the investment, write a provision in the owner's carryback note similar to this one: "No payments shall be made on this note until the Pie-in-the-sky Apartments gross $2,000 per month in rents"—and you could have additional provisions dealing with expenses, work to be done, etc.

This type of provision is known as going with the flow. This provision can minimize the risk of taking on a hungry alligator.

Solution #6 Paper that Walks Backwards

Paper that walks backwards can be very effective in reducing negative cash flow.

About a year ago, I bought a rental house. The owner carried back a $21,000 note that paid $150 per month. The note was to pay ten percent interest. But wait a minute! You math whizzes will realize that the payment doesn't even cover the interest. An interest-only payment would be $175 per month. What happens to the $25 per month interest shortage? It is added on to the principal balance of the loan. The loan balance in this case grows, rather than being reduced by each monthly payment.

In this particular instance, the deal was structured so that it will be due in ten years for approximately $24,000. The loan balance increases with time.

If designed properly, this type of note not only reduces

monthly negative cash flow, but it allows you to not pay interest on the interest shortage amount added on to the loan. In effect, you get the use of the money, in my case $25 per month, for many years *interest free.*

Make sure that the note is written so that you don't pay interest on the accrued interest storage. Only pay interest on the original amount of the loan.

Solution #7   Graduated Payment Loans

Institutional lenders such as banks and savings and loans are glad to help you out with lower payments if Uncle Sam guarantees the loan and in some instances subsidizes the lower monthly payments. This program was established so that young people who couldn't afford stiff monthly payments had an opportunity to buy their own homes.

The program works like this: In the early years of the loan, monthly payments are scheduled to be lower than they would under a normal amortized loan. Then the next few payments would gradually rise. The thinking behind this program is that a couple's income will rise fast enough over the years to handle the increased payment.

For example, a normal twenty-five-year amortized loan for $80,000 at thirteen percent would have a monthly payment of $937.27. If a graduated payment plan were used, the payment in the beginning years of the loan might be interest only of $866.67 per month. That gives Mr. and Mrs. Up and Coming an extra $71 each month. This could be used to service another alligator, save it toward a down payment on another house, or for fix-up money.

These graduated payment programs are generally sponsored by FHA. Check with them for more information.

Solution #8   Share the Alligator

Find an investor who is willing and able to pay your negative cash flows on good properties you find (see Chapter Seventeen on equity sharing).

Jim Eliminates his Alligators

My friend Jim wanted to accumulate fifty houses. He figured that fifty houses would give him the means to retire in five years.

Jim found out that, in his particular real estate market situation, he would have to take on negative cash flow properties to achieve his five-year goal and retire with fifty houses. He had purchased seven or eight houses on his own when he decided that partners would be needed. He found partners who funded the cash down payments and the negative cash flows. Jim found the super deals and managed the properties.

Today, Jim owns forty-five houses. In most of these he is involved with partners who have a fifty percent interest. Jim understands a fundamental principle of real estate empire building: It doesn't do any good to buy millions of dollars in property if you can't hold it long enough for it to grow its money crop.

Solution #9   Share Appreciation with the Seller

Shared appreciation loans from the seller offer a unique method of taming a potential or real alligator.

During negotiations, insist on a lower interest rate. A lower interest rate translates into lower payments and less of a monthly eat. Offer Mr. Seller an eight percent interest rate. If the seller is reluctant to accept such a low interest rate, offer him a percentage of the future profits when you sell.

The profits you share with Mr. Seller might be as low as five percent, or any mutually agreeable figure. The key to making this program work for you is getting a substantial reduction in the prevailing interest rate. The lower payments will help you more comfortably acquire and keep your real estate empire.

The seller gets inflation protection from his loan through the potential appreciation of his home. He might even get a small tax shelter if the deal is properly structured.

I think that this is going to be one of the most important financial tools in real estate for the eighties: Trade off

Solution #9: Share Appreciation with the Seller

REAL ESTATE PURCHASE AGREEMENT
AND RECEIPT FOR DEPOSIT

This is intended to be a legally binding contract. Read it carefully.

_____ , _____ , 19 ____
        (City)   *(State)*

Received from _____
                    (Name)

herein called Buyer, the sum of _____

_____ dollars $ _____ , in the form of cash ☐ ,

cashier's check ☐ personal check ☐ or _____ ☐ payable to
                (Name)
_____ , to be held uncashed

until acceptance of this offer, as deposit on account of purchase price of _____

  sixty thousand _____ dollars $ 60,000.00 _____

for the purchase of property located in _____
                           (City)

County of _____ , _____
       (County)   *(State)*

described as follows: _____
                (Address or other legal description)

Buyer will deposit in escrow with _____
             (Title company or other third party)

the balance of purchase price as follows _____

    1.   Seller agrees to carry first note and deed of trust for
          purchase price of $60,000 payable at 8% interest with
          monthly interest-only payments of $400 for 10 years, at
          which time note is due and payable.

    2.   Seller to retain 5% interest in ownership in property
          and to receive 5% of profits over and above $60,000 when
          property is sold.

Detail above any factual terms and conditions applicable to this sale. such as financing. contingency of sale of other property. the disposition of structural pest control inspection. and repairs and personal property to be included in the sale

Deposit will ☐ will not ☐ be increased by $ _____ to $ _____
within _____ days of acceptance of this offer

Buyer does ☐ does not ☐ intend to occupy subject property as his residence

The supplements initialed below are incorporated as part of this agreement

___ Structural Pest Control Certification Agreement   ___ VA Amendment
___ Special Studies Zone Disclosure   ___ FHA Amendment
___ Flood Insurance Disclosure   ___ Other _____
___ Occupancy Agreement   ___ Other _____

Buyer and Seller acknowledge receipt of a copy of this page. which constitutes page 1 of _____ Pages

X _____   X _____
  Buyer   Seller

X _____   X _____
  Buyer   Seller

small pieces of future profits for more comfortable monthly payments.

Solution #10   Equity for Payments

You might consider offering the seller other real estate and personal properties instead of future or present payments due on a note. These types of items might be an effective alternative solution in backdoor clauses.

You might also consider offering Mr. Lender services such as plumbing, tax preparation, medical, legal, etc. These services could be used in lieu of full or partial payments on a note. Conserve cash, hold real estate, and you will be rich tomorrow.

Solution #11   Single Payment Notes

Try to get Mr. Seller to accept a single payment note. This is one of the most powerful financing techniques you can use to tame that alligator.

A single payment note simply means that Mr. Lender gets only one payment, and that is a balloon at the end of the term of the note. There are no monthly payments. All the interest might be accrued and added on to the principal balance of the note.

Let's say that Mr. Seller is willing to carry back a $20,000 note; you offer the seller a $20,000, ten percent note, with no payments, with the interest to accrue. The principal balance plus accrued interest will be all due in a balloon payment in five years.

What seller would accept this proposition? A motivated seller—we have discussed Mr. Motivation's nonprofit orientation. A seller might see a single payment note as a forced savings program; he might be planning a large expenditure in the future for retirement, children's college, etc.

Try to work for single payment notes whenever you can possibly fit them into a transaction. Being free from making payments on a large portion of an equity is a comfortable way to control a fortune in real estate.

Solution #12   Periodic Payment Note

An alternative to the single payment note is to arrange to have payments made quarterly, semi-annually, or annually. Payments can be interest only. Learn to be inventive, be creative—the terms and provisions of a note are not cast in concrete. Negotiate flexibility at the beginning of a transaction to maximize your future potential profits.

Solution #13   Moratorium on Payments

Ask Mr. Seller for a moratorium on payments for a three-, six-, nine-month or longer period following the close of escrow.

Let's say that you have just found a great rental house in a nice neighborhood. Mr. Seller has agreed to carry back a $20,000 second trust deed at twelve percent interest, with a balloon payment due in five years for the balance of the loan, and monthly interest-only payments of $200.

You have negotiated a key provision in this transaction that will help you turn this deal into a winner. Mr. Seller has agreed to give you a moratorium on payments on the note for six months.

You might say, "That's just (6 × $200 =) $1,200. How will that make this investment a winner?" Let's further assume that you projected that you would have $150 a month negative cash flow; by postponing monthly payments, you could receive a $50 a month positive cash flow ($200 – $150 = $50).

If you set aside the $50-a-month positive cash flow during the six-month moratorium, you can use this money to pay the negative cash flow after the moratorium ends. In effect, you have maintained a neutral cash flow for eight months. Had you arranged a twelve-month moratorium, you could have maintained a neutral cash flow for sixteen months. After this time has passed, you should be able to raise the rents on the house to help reduce the eat. You might even consider structuring another moratorium for a few months at the end of the sixteen-month period.

If you creatively plan ahead, you can find many ways to tame that alligator.

Solution #14   Borrow the Eat

Borrow the cash needed to pay the negative cash flows from a friend, family, or investor on a monthly basis, then arrange to repay them with a future single payment, annually or biannually.

The longer the period before cash comes out of your pocket, the better for you. By putting off repayment dates, two important things are accomplished:

1. You get the negative cash flow handled so that you can control more property comfortably.

2. You give inflation and your creative efforts time to increase property values so that current negative cash flows can be paid with future profits.

This delayed repayment program might provide a high-income friend with a forced savings account. Many people welcome the tax deductions taken by Uncle Sam from their weekly paycheck. They see this as a forced savings program, since many people purposely overpay so that they will receive a later refund. Use this very common motive to attract cash to fund your present negative cash flows.

Solution #15   Options Tame Alligators

Options can be designed to be an effective tool for minimizing or eliminating negative cash flows.

I recently bought a house well below market. My problem was that the house was going to eat $225 per month.

I approached my new tenants and offered them a one-year lease with an option to purchase fifty percent of the house during that year. In exchange, their lease payments would increase $225 and they would take care of all maintenance during the lease period. In order for the lessees to exercise the option for fifty percent of the house, they had to pay me my original cash investment back for acquiring the house, plus a nice cash profit. The option was used to benefit both of us. I handled my alligator, and they harnessed part of the appreciation benefits on the house.

An option is definitely an effective incentive to encourage your tenants to help you out with troublesome negative cash flows.

Solution #16   Seller Feeds Alligator

Have the seller help you with the negative cash flow. There are a lot of Mr. Motivations out there. It is definitely a buyer's market!

If you have used one of the no down payment formulas in which Mr. Motivation has received some cash, you might request that Mr. Motivation subsidize your negative cash flow for $100 per month for, let's say, a two-year period.

Ask for this type of concession during negotiation, and expect to get it! After all, you are solving his problem; it is only right that he should help you with your negative cash flow problems.

This might be implemented at the close of escrow by impounding a specific amount of funds. In this case, two years at $100 per month negative cash flow would mean an impounded balance of $2,400.

An alternative to this procedure would be to have Mr. Motivation buy a trust deed with payments of $100 per month and assign either the note or just twenty-four payments to you.

OTHER METHODS OF PUTTING EATERS ON A DIET

1. Buy lower-priced houses. Houses in lower-income neighborhoods generally command a higher rent relative to market value than those in more affluent areas. These lower-priced houses many times are management headaches, so you will generally earn a more favorable cash flow position.

2. Cut expenses whenever possible. Shop around for insurance. There is no standard rate. When you have a number of properties, use a blanket insurance policy; it will lower this bill considerably. Do maintenance yourself, work to lower tax bills, and basically keep tabs on all costs. Maintain this attitude even when you have grown big, or your real estate empire will be destined to destruction.

3. Rent one house to several singles. This technique works excellently in college towns. By renting out rooms, you can usually command higher rents per house than by renting out the total house to one family.

4. Raise rents by improving property. Paint, carpet, hang new drapes, upgrade the landscaping, etc. William Nickerson's *How I Turned $1,000 into $3,000,000 in Real Estate in My Spare time* thoroughly shows the ins and outs of this technique.

5. Put a Christmas Clause in your lease. The tenant pays a ten percent higher rent for eleven months and gets a moratorium on payments for the twelfth month.

PROVISIONS IN NOTES THAT ENSURE FLEXIBILITY

1. A substitution of collateral clause allows the borrower to give the lender other security for his note. The other security generally must be of equal or greater value than the original security.

For example, let's assume that I owe Mr. Motivation a $20,000 note secured by a deed of trust. In the deed of trust there is a provision that allows me to secure Mr. Motivation's note by other security, i.e., another piece of property, or possibly stocks, bonds, or other trust deeds. At my option, I could substitute different security for Mr. Motivation's note, provided Mr. Motivation's note has at least the same cushion of security as he had before.

This clause gives the real estate builder flexibility in the future to do any of the following:

- Refinance cash out of the property by freeing up more lendable equity.

- Exchange property less the notes, giving a greater equity position for the owner.

- Give another note or security to satisfy the lender's note.

- Move notes off good properties to inventory (non-keepers) properties; this is a method of upgrading the quality of your portfolio.

The substitution of collateral clause generally is written into the trust deed or mortgage and note. It might read like this: "Trustor has the right to substitute collateral of property or paper of greater or equal value." Check with a good real estate attorney when drafting such a clause.

2. We discussed the magic of the subordination clauses for unlocking additional cash in a transaction. Try to negotiate that all owner carryback loans on properties you purchase have a subordination clause for all or some part of the loan. A clause such as this in a trust deed might make a property thousands of dollars more valuable.

3. Ask for a *prepayment discount* clause on notes that you sign. This gives you an opportunity to pay the note off early at something less than the balance owed.

For example, let's assume that you have just signed a $30,000 note that has a prepayment discount provision. It reads as follows: "In the event that the beneficiary elects to sell, assign, or exchange this note or any part thereof, the trustee of same note shall have the first right to purchase that note for seventy-five percent on the existing loan balance."

This particular clause combines the *first right of refusal with the prepayment discount provision.*

What if you negotiated an exclusive right to buy the note for the first year at a fifty percent discount? What have you accomplished?

- You could buy the property and immediately upon the close of escrow exercise the prepayment discount provision. This would significantly reduce the acquisition cost. Better yet, wait a year and then exercise the prepayment provision. Use your cash as long as possible before giving it up.

- You could find a buyer for the seller's note. You arrange to sell the note to the buyer for, let's say,

$25,000; under the discount provision you have the right to buy the note back for $20,000. That's an easy way of making $5,000 cash.

By properly structuring notes at the beginning of a transaction, you can build future flexibility. Building flexibility in your transactions means bigger profits.

THE DETAILS MEAN PROFITS

- Pay attention to the small details of the notes that you sign. Ask for a lower interest rate, no payments, a long repayment term, and all the creative provisions that are necessary for you to make a super deal. Trade these important terms and provisions only for other important concessions.

- Be novel; be creative; design "paper" to solve problems and to maximize profits.

CHAPTER 19
So You Want to Be Your Own Boss

There is going to come a time during your real estate empire building program that you might want to consider quitting your regular nine-to-five job so you can devote all of your energies to building a real estate empire. It will be a time of freedom—no more hurrying off to work in the morning, no more office politics, no more unfair criticisms from your boss, no more boredom! You will be entering the exciting field of real estate investment as a profession, or maybe just taking full-time retirement.

When people ask, "What do you do?" you can answer smugly, "I handle my own investments," or "I'm retired." You've achieved the dream of so many people. To be independent—to make your own hours, to create as much wealth for yourself as you want, rather than for your boss—to pursue the higher goals in life.

John Stuart Mill said, "The only freedom which deserves the name is that of pursuing our own good in our own way."

However, freedom carries with it a greater degree of responsibility. As a full-time real estate investor, you will have critical decisions to make: Do I have enough cash flow from my properties to cover living expenses? Do I have an adequate savings account for emergencies? How will I spend my day? Will I just semi-retire or totally retire? Can I continue to get bank financing for my properties without a regular job? What about insurance? Can I really make it on my own?

Before quitting that secure job, make sure that these questions and others are completely examined, and then create a detailed plan.

PLAN AHEAD

Before you leave that regular paycheck, prepare a detailed written plan of how you intend to live for at least the first year. Having a large real estate net worth will not guarantee that you can pay your phone bill, put gas in the car, or put food on the table.

You need to have cash flow equivalent to the salary that you are leaving, or at least one year's savings in the bank. The time to begin to plan your transition from being a wage slave to self employment is a year in advance.

How Much Do You Need to Live?

A full six months to a year before that blessed day of freedom, start paying more specific attention to your monthly expenditures. Begin keeping a written record of all your personal expenditures during a month. This is called a budget. Let's look at a sample budget.

Gross income		$2,075
Expenses:		
Income taxes*	$ 200	
House payment	500	
Car payments	175	
Food	450	
Clothes	100	
Travel & entertainment	300	
Medical, Dental	75	
Credit card	125	
Miscellaneous	100	
TOTAL		$2,075
SAVINGS		-0-

You are not saving any of your current income! However, if you own, let's say, $300,000 in real estate and it is appreciating at ten percent annually, you are really saving 30,000 nontaxable dollars per year. That's more than your current income. That's not a bad savings plan! You control the real estate money farm; now the key is to hold on to it long enough so that you can turn some of those *future fat equities into spendable cash*.

After you have calculated the amount of money needed to live monthly, prepare an *income-generating plan*. A written plan of this type is vital to your success in making the transition from being a wage slave to a professional real estate investor.

Will you continue to generate $2,075 a month to support your present lifestyle, or would you be willing to

---

*With several pieces of improved real estate, there is still a good chance that you'll be paying much less income taxes. Be sure to sit down with your accountant to see how you need to budget for income taxes.

lower your standard of living temporarily? (I wouldn't recommend raising it right away until you work the bugs out of your self-employment gameplan.)

How might you lower expenses? In the sample budget, the following might be done:

- Pay off car loan prior to freedom

- Pay off credit cards

- Temporarily trim some travel and entertainment expenses

By planning ahead for that magic day of financial freedom, you can pay these bills off a little at a time. Perhaps with your next income tax refund? A Christmas bonus?

Above all, avoid taking on new consumer debts in the planning period. One of the key mistakes a real estate empire builder makes is spending real estate investment profits on consumer items such as boats, airplanes, cars, or a big vacation. This type of consumer mentality will make you a wage slave the rest of your life. Reinvest those profits! A dollar invested wisely will grow in value. A dollar spent on a consumer item is gone!

Yes, you might enjoy those items now; but put that "now" enjoyment off for a few short years and you will be able to have your money work for you rather than you work for your money. The airplanes and exotic cars will come, if that is what you want. Just give it time!

Create Cash Reserves

Let's look at some common ways in which a real estate empire builder develops cash reserves in anticipation of being self-employed.

- Refinance one or more properties

- Take money out of a retirement fund

- Cash in a life insurance policy

- Borrow from a credit union, a friend, a family member

- Get a part-time real estate consulting service going and save income

- Be a real estate agent part-time and save

- Build up a portfolio of notes paying monthly income

- Sell part of property to investors for cash

- Put a systematic savings program into effect

- Be a loan broker part-time, and save

- Buy and sell inventory property, and save the profits

- Trade properties for income producers, i.e., notes, apartments, etc.

One of the most important parts of the transition period to self-employment is the building of some cash reserves. Make sure that once you quit you won't need to come begging back to that old job in six months.

THE FIVE-YEAR RETIREMENT PLAN

One of the best techniques I know for creating a lifetime income involves refinancing your properties.

Let's say that you have been buying well-selected pieces of residential income property for five years. You have purchased these properties at a very moderate pace—one house per year—so that you now own five houses.

Let's look at your real estate portfolio.

	House #1	House #2	House #3	House #4	House #5
Market Value	$75,000	$65,000	$80,000	$79,000	$85,000
Loans	$30,000	$33,000	$50,000	$61,000	$70,000
Equity	$45,000	$32,000	$30,000	$18,000	$15,000

Congratulations! With a minimum of effort, you have acquired a real estate net worth of $140,000. You are way ahead of most people!

You have decied that you want to have more free time to just relax, to pursue a larger real estate empire, etc. It is time to quit that nine-to-five drudgery. "How will I live?" you ask. In most cases, Mr. Local Grocer won't take real estate equities for food (although you might try).

You could sell one of your houses, but that's like selling the money farm; it keeps growing new equities each season. The empire building program is based on buying and holding well-selected real estate.

Why don't you refinance one of the houses just before quitting your job? Let's assume that you refinance House #1. You apply, and receive from your local friendly savings and loan a new $60,000 loan payable at $656.61 per month, at thirteen percent interest. You are now receiving $500 per month rent. You now have a negative cash flow of ($156.62 + $75.00 taxes and insurance =) $231.61.

What benefits are you getting for changing a property with a cash flow into an eater?

New loan	$60,000
Pay off old loan	30,000
Gross loan proceeds	30,000
Less loan costs	1,500
Net cash in your pocket	$28,500

From the approximately $28,500 in cash generated by refinancing, you take $5,000 and place it in a money market fund or other liquid savings account. This money can be withdrawn on a monthly basis to service your negative cash flow on the refinanced property for a couple of years.

The other $23,500 in funds could also be placed in a separate high-yielding money market fund, savings plan, etc. You could then draw this money out at the rate of $2,000 per month to take care of one year's living expenses (the $500 shortage should be made up by the interest earned on the average balance of funds deposited).

With a little creative planning, you have just raised one year's cash needs. One year of freedom to pursue a more aggressive real estate acquisition program—or just to lie under a shade tree snoozing. It will be your choice! You'll think back on your choice to buy that nice little rental house five years before with a smile. You never believed that one little house could grow a large enough cash crop to give you a full year of freedom.

What do you do the second year? Your second house should have grown enough equity for you to refinance it. Each year you should be able to refinance another house. What happens at the end of five years? House #1 should have grown a new money crop; harvest it and continue to live off of your real estate investments. Another added bonus is that money refinanced out of a property is *tax-free* cash.

If you need or want more income, plan to buy two or three or more houses per year. Just think, if you quit your job owning twenty houses, by using this technique you could generate almost $100,000 per year income—tax-free!

To buy four houses a year for five years is actually very simple, if you work consistently in your spare time. I mean just ten to fifteen hours per month. I have personally bought four houses in one day. You can certainly do it in one year.

I recently heard of a fellow who owns 15,000 houses. Try to calculate what his annual income might be if he employed the refinancing technique!

KEEPERS AND INVENTORY—THE DIVIDED PORTFOLIO

Many professional real estate investors have their property divided into two categories:

- Keepers
- Inventory

A *keeper* is a well-located piece of real estate that has long-term potential to appreciate with minimal effort on your part. A nice single-family home located in an attractive and upwardly mobile neighborhood is my idea of a *keeper*.

Inventory is a property that an investor buys with the specific intention of reselling at a quick profit. Houses and apartments in lower-income areas, inner-city areas, and deteriorating neighborhoods are on my inventory list. Specifically, any property that requires excessive management responsibility is inventory.

CASH FLOW FROM INVENTORY

How can you create cash flow from inventory? Find properties that are undervalued. These types of properties generally need paint, cleanup, and maybe some drapes and carpeting. You can usually fix up a building of this sort for less money than the discounted price justified. Then resell this type of property for a quick profit.

John's Quick Profit

My friend John recently found a one-bedroom house for sale. The owner was asking $20,000. The owner had become a classic Mr. Motivation. When John met him at the house, the sewer had just backed up. Mr. Motivation was fed up with the day-to-day repairs and management the house required.

John was able to buy the house for $16,000 with $1,000 down. The owner carried a low-interest first trust deed for the balance of the purchase price. John spent a couple of hundred dollars to cure the sewer plug-up and clean up the property. He resold it the next day for a $3,000 net cash profit. Both transactions took about three hours. In three hours John made $3,000, or $1,000 an hour—because he knew the market and acted quickly.

With one transaction like this a month, you could generate enough cash flow to cover living expenses.

What else could John have done? He could have sold the house for a higher price, let's say $25,000 for no money down; he could have carried back a high-monthly-payment second trust deed, for example, a $10,000 second trust deed payable at $100 per month.

You don't have to be a math whiz to figure out that by making a few of these deals a year, you could build a pretty healthy monthly income in a short time.

Buying low and selling high is probably one of the most common ways the professional real estate investor generates cash flow.

The Sandwich Lease

The sandwich lease is another excellent way to develop a consistent monthly cash flow.

My friend Jim recently came across a business opportunity, a donut shop that was going out of business. Jim found out that the lease on the building in which the donut shop was located presented a nice cash flow opportunity.

The monthly payment on the lease was $65. The term of the lease was scheduled to run four more years, with an option to renew for an additional five years at $85 per month.

Jim checked around and discovered that comparable space was renting for $350. Jim immediately offered the owner of the donut shop $4,000 for his business, including the lease. Jim borrowed the $4,000, so that he had none of his own money invested. The offer was accepted.

He immediately found a tenant and sublet the space for $350. His lease payment was $65. His cash flow from his sandwich lease each month was $285.

How did Jim pay back the $4,000? He sold the equipment from the donut shop for $1,500 cash. He gave that to his lender friend; in addition, he gave his friend a small chunk of equity in one of his rental houses.

What were some of the other alternatives available to Jim?

- Assign part of the sandwich lease cash flow to the lender to amortize the loan

- Sell his cash flow for cash to investor

- Exchange the entire cash flow with someone who has saleable personal property

- Substitute a lower monthly payment note secured by one of his properties to satisfy the lender's debt. For example, he could give the lender a single payment note due in five years.

The sandwich opportunity is available in your area. Look at the "Business Opportunities For Sale" section of your newspaper; talk to auctioneers; and check the bankruptcies and "Commercial Space For Lease" columns of your newspaper. This is an excellent idea for generating cash flow.

Cash Flow Units

You may be fortunate enough to have cash flow from your properties. Generally, it reflects a large equity position in the property.

Are large equity positions in a property always a result of a long holding period? Not necessarily. Let's look at other ways of increasing equity and cash flow in a shorter time period:

- Upgrade property and raise rents

- *Walk* loans off of one property to another and sell the other property. (This is called definancing)

- Put property to a higher and better use, e.g., residential to commercial

- Improve management operations

- Exchange properties geographically to areas that still have low equity cash flow properties.

Guard that cash flow from your property. You will need to become a more vigilant manager—no more letting rent collections slide until the fifteenth of the month.

I had some cash flow from my units when I quit my job. However, because I became so busy pursuing those pie-in-the-sky deals, I loosened my management operations, and as a result found that my cash flow suffered.

If you feel that you can find great deals, manage your property, and still have those kicking-back, relaxing times, that's great! That's the mark of a true empire builder.

I decided to hire a manager. When the time comes in your investment life to hire a manager, choose very carefully! A good manager can free you from the day-to-day problems of property ownership; a bad one can not only add to the aggravations, but jeopardize your real estate empire.

Lease-Options—A Cash Flow Management Tool

The lease-option is a wonderful technique for transforming an alligator into a property that has cash flow. Let's say that you have some good strong tenants in one of your rental houses. The tenants are good, but the property has a negative cash flow of $100 per month.

You sit down with Mr. and Mrs. Goode Tenant and go over the benefits of owning real estate. You offer to give Mr. and Mrs. Goode Tenant an option to purchase a fifty-percent interest in the house at today's price. In exchange, you would like their lease payments to be increased by $200 per month. The current rent is $400 per month.

You might structure it in the following manner:

- You give Mr. and Mrs. Goode Tenant a two year lease-option.

- Lease payments the first year would be $600 per month.

- Lease payments the second year would be $700 per month.

- The option has two key elements in it:

  1. If lease payment is received after the fifth of any month, the option becomes void.

  2. The lessees deliver a sum of cash in two years equal to fifty percent of the equity at the current

value (this could be based on an appraisal), in order to buy a fifty percent interest in the property.

Make sure that you consult with a competent real estate attorney prior to making any contract of this type.

This formula is a double winner! You turn an alligator into cash flow, and Mr. and Mrs. Goode Tenant start harnessing the great appreciation benefits of real estate.

JOBS RELATED TO YOUR EMPIRE BUILDING EFFORTS

When I first quit my job, I took some time off to travel, to meditate, and to generally take it easy. I had my one year's income snug in the bank, and my real estate portfolio was showing a nice cash flow.

After some lazy time, I decided to find ways in which I could generate more cash flow. I wanted to do this so that I could continue to pyramid my estate. I wasn't ready for retirement.

In my experience of investing, I had cultivated various sources of short-term and long-term funds. These lenders included loan brokers, financing companies, and occasionally an insurance company.

People were continually coming to me asking where they might get loans—firsts, seconds, thirds, wrap-arounds—and where to sell trust deeds, etc. I would simply refer them directly to my sources.

One day, I decided that I should get paid for finding money. I became a part-time money finder. It's a very simple business. Call your local loan brokers and finance companies and ask the following questions:

1. Do you give referral fees?

2. What is the interest rate charged on loans?
   • Owner-occupied?
   • Commercial?
   • Nonowner-occupied?

3. What are the repayment schedules? Three years, five years, thirty years, etc.

4. What types of monthly repayment programs do you have?
   - Interest only
   - Amortized
   - Balloon payments

5. What credit requirements do you have?

6. What information do you need to process the loan?

7. How many points do you charge?

Once you have this information, place an ad in your local newspaper (check the local laws in regard to the legality of your advertising).

Here is an example of an ad I have used:

MONEY FOR SALE
$5,000 to $1,000,000
Fast service from private party.
Call Ed at 000-000-0000

Sure, you're competing with the local loan brokers; but you will find that many people would rather deal with a private party than with a large mortgage company.

As you receive calls, you can do one of several things. Screen the prospective borrowers to find out if they meet minimum lending requirements for your lenders. If they don't qualify, they still might be good candidates for selling their property, or perhaps an option might solve their problem. Use the no down payment formulas and come to the prospective borrowers' rescue. It's your job!

If you decide that they qualify for a loan through one of your sources, then you can do one of two things:

1. Get them to give you all the necessary paperwork.

2. Get the prospective borrower's name and number, then contact the lender and have him do all the selling and process the paperwork.

Be sure to get a written agreement between you and the borrower detailing what you'll get as a fee when the loan is successfully approved.

Whenever I've used this finder's technique, I've consistently made $2,000 per month with a very minor time commitment. Generally, you can expect between one and three percent of the loan to be your fee.

It is a good method of generating cash flow and prospecting for Mr. Motivation.

Buying and Selling Notes

Another method a money finder can use to generate cash flow involves buying trust deeds. The idea is to buy the trust deed or mortgage at a low price and resell it at a higher price.

To do this effectively, you need to know how to calculate yields. The yield on a note is determined by three main factors:

- Monthly payments

- Length of the loan. Is there a balloon payment?

- Interest rate on the face of the note

A good financial calculator can help you compute yields very quickly. The higher the yield you desire, the lower the price you would pay for a note, and thus the larger the discount would be.

For example, I was approached recently to buy a note with a $15,000 balance owing. The payments on the note were $150 per month and the interest rate was twelve percent. There would be a balloon payment of $15,000 in two years, since the payments only covered the interest. I offered the seller of the note $11,143. I was willing to make this offer, because I knew that an investor would pay approximately $12,643 for the note. That would give Mr. Investor a fat twenty-two percent yield on his money.

I purchased the note and did sell it to Mr. Investor. My fee was the difference between what I paid for it, $11,143 and the amount for which I sold it, $12,643. In this transaction, I earned $1,500 for a couple of hours work. Learn to employ these types of techniques to work less—to work smarter—so that you can be free of cash flow problems while you acquire that real estate empire.

One final word about buying and selling trust deeds: Protect your investor!

- Check out the properties on which the note exists.

- Make sure that there is an adequate equity cushion in case you have to foreclose in the future.

- Get title insurance as an endorsement to the existing title policy.

- Make sure that Mr. Investor is named loss payee in the property's insurance policy. Your investors are very vital assets in empire building—protect them!

- A good book to learn more about this technique is entitled *How to Grow a Money Tree*. It was written by Dave Glubetich and is published by Impact Publishing Company in San Ramon, California.

Flexible Related Part-Time Jobs

Real Estate Agent. This can give you periodic bunches of cash and expose you to some hot new deals, but to be good at this job means putting in long hours. If you do this type of work, try to find a comfortable balance between building your empire and generating cash flow. Don't make the mistake of working full-time for your money again; make your money work full-time for you.

Teach Real Estate Courses. Nothing solidifies the knowledge of any field more than teaching it. There is a big demand for these courses today at local colleges and adult schools. After all, most people's wealth is tied up in their real estate.

Property Management. If you are organized and have the emotional stamina and tenacity, this can be a fine cash flow generator. You will also be exposed to many super deals before they hit the market!

Real Estate Consultant. Get paid for what you know. Help "For sale by owner" type people structure a beneficial sale. Let your local realtors know that you are available to help solve buyer-seller financial problems.

DO YOU NEED AN OFFICE?

No! Work at home if at all possible your first year. If you have distractions from your family, just grind your teeth and growl. They'll get the message. Besides, most of the time you should be out beating the bushes for super deals.

Remember, your first year on your own is a new experience. Keep your overhead as low as possible. It is easy to get carried away with a self-deluded big-shot image. All your former colaborers will bow at your feet by admiring your courage. Everybody sees you as rich. You see yourself as rich. That's good! Just don't act like it with your pocketbook quite yet. A year on your own will give you a good track record and some momentum! Then you can find a more extravagant and personally desirable niche.

After all, can you imagine how you would feel crawling back to your old job? You would be ashamed. More importantly, you would have let down those people who worshipped your courage. You would have shattered their dream of "Someday, I might do that." Everybody needs a dream. Don't shatter their dream.

GOALS AND YOUR TIME

You're on your own! Freedom! Along with freedom comes responsibility. With some people, freedom represents just enough rope to financially hang themselves. How will you handle your newfound financial freedom? Sleep in, travel, play tennis, read, occasionally make a deal. Pretty vague; vague plans can create a vague future. Get specific!

For at least your first year of self-employment (after a well-deserved vacation or goofing-off period), structure your day as though you had a job. In fact, you do have a job. The real difference is that you will be getting all the fruits of your efforts, instead of just scraps. You'll be working for yourself.

Get up early and plan your daily schedule. It's easy to space out and quit working early to go swimming or just lie in the sun. There will be plenty of time for all of this type of play when you've proven that you can make it on your own.

One year of working full-time on your own investments might be worth three or four years working part-time.

That first year on your own is a vital link between your wage slave days and true financial freedom. Write your retirement plan today; put down every detail; begin to create your financial future. Work your plan so that your money will be working for you, and don't look back.

CHAPTER 20
Strategies for the Future

As Bob Dylan said in his famous folk ballad of the '60s, "The times, they are a-changin'." The seventies brought to us extraordinary profits in real estate. Why? Because Uncle Sam insisted on flooding the market with his paper dollar bills. This is the fundamental cause of inflation.

Buying an essential commodity such as real estate with its unique capability for being leveraged harnessed the engine of inflation to create fortunes in the seventies.

In this book, I have given you the investment tools so that you can ride the crest of inflation, rather than be victimized by it. You can create a real estate empire in the future. However, the eighties have brought some new rules to the game. These new rules have created new opportunities, as well as some new potential pitfalls.

The fundamental factors continue. Even with the lower inflation rates of the eighties, real estate in areas of good economic growth is rising steadily in value. If inflation accelerates, as some economists predict, then real estate might rise faster than inflation. (This will happen as people become more aware of how quickly their paper currency is declining in value and seek alternative storehouses of value for their wealth.) I think that inflation will continue. Barring any Hoover-like mistakes by the powers in the White House, I see inflation ranging in the next five years between a low of five percent and a high of fifteen percent. In my mind, there is a better chance of it being in the high end of this range than in the low end.

What changes can we expect in the eighties?

- New forms of financing

- New formulas for coping

- New investment trends

- Increased risks

FINANCIAL TOOLS FOR THE EIGHTIES

The real estate doomsayers admit that there is a tremendous backlog of demand for houses; however, they maintain that the primary reason for the phenomenal appreciation of housing prices in the seventies was cheap long-term mortgage money. Right! But even when cheap long-term mortgage money is not available from traditional institutional sources, such as savings and loans, if you bargain effectively, Mr. Seller still might be willing to carry back long-term, fixed-rate, low-interest, level-payment loans.

The banking and savings and loan industries depend on those of us who borrow money for real estate purchases for their very survival. Those who have money become very inventive when they are threatened with losing it. However, where there is a need, it must be filled.

I am pleased to announce to the doomsayers of real state that the big money people, those innovative money merchants (banks, savings and loans, insurance companies) have designed some neat little programs that will allow people to borrow at acceptable terms even in times of high interest rates. Some of the benefits of ownership may be shifted from the owner to the lender, but of course, real estate is such a great investment vehicle that it is okay if we share a little of our good fortune. All of us will be happier.

The new types of loans are designed with inflation in mind. I repeat, if inflation continues and increases, well-selected real estate is an incomparable investment if financed properly, and even if inflation stabilizes, well-selected real estate with properly designed financing, purchased below market value, has no equal at creating wealth for the average person. Now, let's look and see how Mr. Money Merchant is going to help us build our real estate empire in the eighties.

New Lending Packages

The adjustable rate mortgages, or A.R.M.s as they are called in the industry, appear to be the cure-all for the lenders' inflation woes.

Basically, the A.R.M. comes in two brands. Brand X, offered by "We Want Some of It" Savings and Loan allows the lender to change the interest rate either up or down within specific limits.

It might work like this: You have applied for and received an A.R.M. from your local "We Want Some of It" Savings and Loan. The amount of the loan will be $75,000, carrying an initial interest rate of thirteen percent, amortized over thirty years. In the terms of your agreement, there is a provision that allows the lender to adjust the interest rate up or down within a five percent limit; in this case, that means that the rate could go as high as eighteen percent or as low as eight percent. The adjustment might be made according to some predetermined (by the lender) cost of funds or other financial index. Usually with this type of loan the lender might only readjust the rate on a periodic basis, such as quarterly, semi-quarterly, or annually.

The danger of a loan like this is that your monthly payments could vary considerably. For example, if you took out an A.R.M. loan of $75,000 at thirteen percent interest, your original monthly payment would be $820.76. If the rate on the A.R.M. loan rose to eighteen percent, the increased payment might jump to $1,113.61 per month. That is a $292.85 per month increase. Of course, if interest rates fall, you get a lower payment.

In effect, you are sharing part of the appreciation benefits of owning your own home or property with "We Want Some of It" Savings and Loan. If you are going to use their money to profit in real estate, the money merchants want you to assume some of the risk of inflation, and they intend to share in some of its rewards.

The problem with this program is that your monthly payment could very well jump at a faster rate than your wages or rental income. You might be in jeopardy of losing the property.

The good news is that "We Want Some of It" Savings and Loan might be willing to lend you money at a lower-than-market interest rate.

The range within which the lender can adjust the interest rate is fixed; he cannot raise it above that point for thirty years. This element tends to limit your risk.

Many lenders are beginning to implement this program. Without increasing monthly payments, or only increasing them slightly, Mr. Banker might be willing to add any interest shortages onto the balance of the loan. That means you might have a balloon payment at some future date, either when you sell, or at some specific time.

If this is the method that the lenders choose to handle the interest shortages, it makes the A.R.M. a program that I think consumers will accept. I personally don't think a balloon payment thirty years down the road is going to damage the real estate market very much, unless of course the balloon payment of the loan exceeds the value of the property. Be careful!

These negatively amortized loans (where the loan balance increases with each payment) have become popular in the last year with builders who are seducing would-be homebuyers with first-year interest rates and payments at eight percent and nine percent. However, "there ain't no such thing as a free lunch." In the fine print, many of these adjustable rate loans will jump from an eight percent negatively amortized loan in the first year to a thirteen and a half percent positively amortized loan in the second or third year. Your payment could jump hundreds of dollars witin a short period of time, giving you beads of sweat on your upper lip while you're trying to figure out how you'll make the higher payment.

Unlimited A.R.M.

The second type of A.R.M. deals with rates that can be adjusted without limit. "I Want It All" Savings and Loans are fashioning these types of loans. For example, if you sign an unlimited A.R.M. thirty-year note today, and the cost of money rose substantially, you might be paying a thirty percent interest rate or more a couple of years from now.

The unlimited adjustable rate mortgage shifts most of the home ownership benefits to the lender. If mortgage rates skyrocket, you have but a couple of unacceptable investment options.

- You could be at risk to make higher and higher payments or face foreclosure.

- You could have ever-rising interest shortages added on to your original loan balance. This could eliminate a large portion, if not all, of the equity you might have accumulated.

Many of these A.R.M. programs provide the buyer with up to six months to sell the property upon notification of all interest rate changes before the rate actually jumps. However, what happens if the rate jumps eight points? Who would be willing to buy your house? You definitely need some safeguards.

This sort of economic uncertainty would add, in my opinion, some unacceptable risks to property ownership. You might have two identical properties side by side on the same street with significantly different market values. Why? Because of the financing. One might have an A.R.M. with an unlimited swing in the interest rate, while the other might have a long-term fixed loan. Which one would you buy?

Stay away from the unlimited A.R.M. If you need an institutional mortage, an A.R.M. with a limited interest rate adjustment may be your best bet. A little later in this chapter, I'll show you how to limit your risk when using A.R.M.s.

Shared Appreciation Mortgages (S.A.M.)

Shared appreciation mortages, or S.A.M.s, as they are called in the industry, are basically a partnership between the lender and the borrower. Each party can benefit. Briefly, it works like this: The prospective homebuyer (investor) gets a lower-than-market interest rate from his "Let's Be Fair About This" Savings and Loan. In exchange, the homeowner (investor) gives up part of his potential profits at the time of sale. The future date of sale would be agreed upon at the loan origination date.

What happens if you don't want to sell your house at the preagreed date? You will probably have to get an appraisal at that date and arrange to pay off the lender's share of the increased equity in your home. Where would you get the money to pay off "Let's Be Fair About It" Savings and Loan? Generally, there are refinance provisions in the agreement at current rates to fund the savings and loan payoff.

Real estate investment is like a money farm. It grows a

new money crop each year. With S.A.M.s, you are just sharing the money crop. You become an equity sharecropper with the lender. You get lower holding costs, let us say possibly a nine percent interest rate instead of fourteen percent, and the lender gets some of the appreciation benefits of property ownership.

I think that loans of this type can fill the void of financing in the inflationary eighties. You don't get all the benefits of the enormous potential appreciation in real estate, but for many of you this is a reasonable way to get started on a limited budget.

Remember, while you're building that real estate empire, don't minimize the importance of holding costs. They are a critical factor in your pursuit of real estate wealth. If you have to turn to Mr. Money Merchant, I think that S.A.M.s can be a beneficial way to finance property purchases in the eighties.

Renegotiable Rate Mortgages (R.R.M.)

Basically, this type of loan is written for thirty years, with a preset date on which to renegotiate the interest rate, say every five years. The word renegotiate suggests that you have a negotiable choice as to what interest rate you might pay at a specified future date. Where is the choice? Go to five different banks in your area and compare the different interest rates they charge. There is not a significant difference. In the event general interest rates skyrocket to, let's say thirty percent over the next five years, what bargaining latitude do you suppose Mr. Borrower will have when his loan comes up for renegotiation? Perhaps he'll find a bargain-rate loan at twenty-eight percent. That's too much risk for me.

These types of loans are similar to the unlimited A.R.M.s. The borrower virtually has no choice; he'll be forced to pay a considerably higher rate when the loan comes up for renegotiation if interest rates stay high.

If there is a reasonable upside limit set to the new renegotiated rate, then these loans show some promise. In effect, by establishing a reasonable upward limit to a

future renegotiated interest rate, you will be sharing a
portion of the appreciation in the property with the lender.
What is a reasonable upward limit to interest rates? That
will depend on your total circumstances—income, future
income, acquisition cost of property. I personally would
generally not accept any rate that exceeded five percent
over the original rate charged. Always try to find a way to
limit your risk with these new types of loans.

Equity Sharing

Equity sharing programs can be a very beneficial financing
tool for real estate empire building. See Chapter Seventeen for a more complete discussion. These will be an
important financial tool if used properly in the eighties.
More group ownership of real estate will occur in the
eighties; to achieve your success you'll need to fully understand the ins and outs of group ownership.

Other New Lending Programs

- Graduated payments
- Amortized loan with a balloon payment after three
  to five years
- Principal increases with the cost of living index

The primary purpose for these new types of loans is to
allow Mr. Money Merchant the opportunity to reap some
of the benefits of inflation rather than be victimized by it.
Your challenge is to keep as many of the appreciation
goodies inflation bestows on real estate as possible. Limit
the range within which any variable rate loan may fluctuate.

CHALLENGES OF THE EIGHTIES

The eighties have brought new sets of challenges to those
of us who want to build our empire in real estate. With
each new challenge, there comes a golden opportunity.
Unlock the riddle to the challenge and you will be rich
beyond your wildest dreams.

Let's look at some possible keys that can unlock those riddles and challenges for you.

Coping with Adjustable Rate Mortgages

1. Negative fixed wrap-around mortgage. What a mouthful! It is critical to maximizing profits in real estate that you obtain some degree of long-term certainty with financing on your properties. You want to be certain that your interest rate will remain fixed, or within a fixed range, for a long period of time. Let's say that you find what appears to be an outstanding buy on a nice rental house, but you discover that the loan on the house is an unlimited A.R.M. What do you do? Walk away? Maybe. Mr. Seller has a monumental problem; as an ambitious real estate empire builder, your fortune depends upon solving his problems. How can you help?

The seller is asking $90,000. This price is below the cost of comparable houses in the area that have fixed-rate long-term loans. The A.R.M. loan balance is $60,000; the present interest rate is fifteen percent. Remember, an unlimited A.R.M. has no upside limit to the interest rate. Simply stated, the problem is this: How do you fix the rate of the loan for the longest term possible?

This guy is really motivated, so you have a live Mr. Motivation. You offer the seller $10,000 down and have him carry back a wrap-around mortgage of $80,000 at sixteen percent interest, amortized over thirty years. (These high interest rate figures are only used for examples. I personally won't sign a note that has an interest rate over thirteen percent, fixed rate or not! This figure might change if the inflation rate changes significantly, up or down.) You make the balance of the seller's equity in the form of a wrap-around mortgage all due with a balloon payment in ten years.

What have you accomplished? By giving the seller a premium of one percent over the current rate (sixteen percent instead of fifteen percent) he is paying on the A.R.M., you are able to obtain a fixed payment for ten years. If the interest rate on the underlying A.R.M. rises above sixteen percent, then the seller (or whoever holds the wrap) must take money out of his pocket each month to service the increase in the underlying note payment.

Also, the wrap-around loan might be written so that any interest shortages will reduce the beneficiary's (Mr. Motivation's) equity in the wrap first. This gives you a $20,000 cushion ($80,000 wrap − $60,000 underlying loan = $20,000 cushion) for absorbing interest shortages, since this is Mr. Motivation's total equity in the wrap—and thus reduces your risk in buying a property with an unlimited A.R.M. The risk is significantly shared by Mr. Motivation. Let's see how the numbers work on this:

- *Underlying first loan:* 1st trust deed $60,000 at fifteen percent over thirty years payable at $758.67 per month.

- *Wrap-around loan:* $80,000 at sixteen percent over thirty years.

Wrap-around payment	$1,075.81
1st loan payment	− 758.67
Net to the seller each month	$ 317.14

If the underlying interest rate on the loan went up to twenty percent, then the underlying loan payment would go to $1,002.61.

Your payment is fixed	$1,075.81
	−1,002.61
Net monthly proceeds to the seller	$ 73.20

Mr. Motivation's net cash flow started at $317.14. If interest rates went to twenty percent as in our example, his cash flow would be reduced to $73.20. If interest rates went higher yet, Mr. Motivation might have to use the remainder of his cash flow to cover the increased monthly payment. If higher interest rates cause payments to exceed Mr. Motivation's cash flow, then any additional payments you have to make might become a direct reduction of his wrap equity. You have just transferred most of the risk of having an unlimited adjustable rate mortage from you to Mr. Motivation.

Negotiate hard for the fixed-rate term loans; if this ploy doesn't work, repackage the loan so that the risk of skyrocketing future interest rates is shared by Mr. Motivation in some manner—and be sure to adjust the purchase price accordingly.

Let's look at some more ways of keeping that payment fixed.

2. If you get involved in an A.R.M. on a house or other piece of property, try selling fifty percent or more of your equity in the house to an investor. He might give you cash and/or an agreement that he will handle any increase in payments. You might have to offer some nice incentives for an investor to participate in this type of transaction. These could include a larger share of ownership, more tax benefits, more profits at the end, or a guaranteed return.

3. Have the seller indemnify you against an interest rate rise. At the close of escrow, have the seller place in a trust account a sum of cash. A trustee might be given instructions to release a specific amount of cash to you if the interest rate on the A.R.M. loan you assumed rose to a predetermined rate.

THE RETURN OF FIXED-RATE MORTGAGES

In the mid-eighties, as interest rates fell to more moderate levels, we saw once again the underlying popularity of fixed-rate mortgages. Once the interest rate on fixed-rate mortgages fell below the twelve to thirteen percent level, more and more homebuyers selected fixed-rate loans, even though they had to pay a little higher interest rate than they would have paid on adjustable-rate mortgages.

Given the opportunity to choose, most people will still go for fixed-rate mortgages rather than all the fancy new types of mortgages that bankers dreamed up in the early eighties. That is why I advise everyone to get a fixed-rate loan if you can. A fixed-rate loan on your house will always make your house easier to sell if you should ever decide to do so. And if you keep your house, that fixed rate is a guarantee that your house payments will always stay manageable . . . even if inflation returns to its high level of past years.

And what will happen to A.R.M.s and S.A.M.s and R.R.M.s and all those other three-letter words? I think they are with us to stay. Whenever interest rates are low or even moderate, they will not be popular. But when the interest rate cycle turns upwards again, they will be the only kind of loan that many people will be able to qualify for.

I hope that, having read this far, you will understand how much better it is to avoid all this financing whenever possible. Go to the place that offers the lowest interest rates, the most flexible terms, and often the lowest down payment. Where is that place? Why, it's the home of the motivated seller. Let the seller provide your financing!

Even though depreciation write-offs must now be taken over a longer time period and there are limits on the setting-off of ordinary income against real estate investment write-offs, real estate investments still provide the best tax shelter and investment combination available in America. The tax law changes have caused the real estate empire builder to shift his attention from tax benefits to a new emphasis on positive cash flow. It is even more important to buy below market value and to have flexible financing arrangements. Lease options, sandwich leases, foreclosures, and fixer-uppers are some examples of the techniques that are especially useful for the new challenges facing the real estate empire builder. No matter what changes take place in the future, creative techniques and solutions will always make real estate a winner. Well-selected real estate with properly designed financing, purchased below market value, has no equal at creating wealth for the average person.

CHAPTER 21
Investment Winners of the Future

You are now a bona fide problem solver. You have the ideas necessary to buy property for no down payment; you've learned how to tame that alligator; you're charged and ready to go. Now it's time to figure out what the best form of real estate investment will be for the next five years.

During the seventies, there was a very simple formula for making money in real estate: Buy it, hold it, and sell it. People made money on almost any type of real estate they bought.

In the next five years, the same type of formulas will work, except that you'll have to pay more attention to the type of real estate you buy and pay more particular attention to the financing of the property.

The key to real estate investment success in the eighties will be to buy as much as you can of the *right kind of property*, with the *right kind of financing*, and hold it. This simple formula will be the basis for your real estate empire.

WHAT CHANGES CAN WE EXPECT?

My crystal ball tells me that economic trends, costly bureaucratic rules, higher land costs, home video and computer systems, and more people working at home will necessitate widespread changes in the expectations people have for their housing.

People will gradually accept smaller houses with fewer amenities. There will be more of an emphasis on condominium and cooperative housing, e.g., senior citizen homes, mobile home parks, halfplexes, and townhouses, as well as housing clusters formed by people of common philosophical and religious bonds. There will be households doubling up and inventive builders who address the special needs that two families have when living in one house. Also, there will be more renters and less homeownership.

As demand rises for this type of housing, more money will flow into these basic shelter dwellings, and prices will rise.

My crystal ball also tells me that people will be willing to spend a higher portion of their income for housing. In some parts of western Europe, as much as sixty percent of a household's gross income is spent to provide adequate shelter. In the United States, approximately thirty to thirty-five percent of a family's gross income may be spent on housing. There is definite room to trade off that Big Mac at lunch each day for a higher house payment.

The real estate builder's philosophy is based on buying shelter—income-producing real estate such as single family houses, condominiums, townhouses, duplexes, four-plexes. I think that these will be the star real estate investment vehicles of the eighties. Larger apartment buildings, in my opinion, face some risky problems, e.g., rent control. Let's look at the investment winners of the eighties in more detail.

WHAT IS A GOOD REAL ESTATE INVESTMENT IN THE EIGHTIES?

1. Single family houses located in areas with a good economic base. Houses have been, and I think will continue to be, investment winners of the eighties. Why? Because there is an obvious fundamental need for them. People need shelter! Also, the single family home represents something beyond shelter in America. The space and the life-style that people have enjoyed with the single family home is something that won't be given up easily.

Sure, it is difficult for many people to afford houses today, given the current economic climate, high interest rates, and cost to build new housing. However, because of the increasing cost of travel, more jobs being located in the home, and the high priority people give to their housing in this country, my feeling is that more people will opt for nicer living accommodations at the expense of travel, entertainment, etc.

Let's look at other reasons I think that the single family home will be tops.

Inflation

As the cost of materials to build houses rises, so house prices rise; as government red tape and thus time delays increase for new developments, the cost of building moves relentlessly upwards. These factors translate into higher prices for the would-be homebuyer.

There has never been a period in recorded history when housing and inflation didn't go up together. Now is the time to buy!

Liquidity

I've always found it easier to get a loan on my houses than on apartments. Lenders generally feel more comfortable and will lend you more money on houses. It's usually easier to sell a house than a large apartment building. There are simply more buyers; thus, more demand.

Diversification

If you own houses that are in different neighborhoods and perhaps in different cities, you minimize the risk of being financially wiped out by an economic or natural disaster (such as a tornado), or having the largest employer in town move out.

If I have a fifteen-unit apartment building and natural or economic disaster strikes, I'm in real trouble! I could lose my entire investment. I would much rather have 'fifteen houses scattered in different locations. Work to minimize your investment risks through diversification.

Management

My experience has been that you get a much higher quality and more permanent tenant in houses. Also, these tenants will sometimes handle maintenance problems for you. Generally, if you're careful in the tenant selection process, a house renter pays more promptly with less hassle.

RENT CONTROL IS COMING!

Normally, rent control is not a large consideration with rental houses. As inflation continues to charge forward, there's going to be increasing pressure from the misguided do-gooders to put limits on the amount a landlord can increase rents.

The main thrust of widespread rent control will be on apartments. There is a high probability that some form of widespread rent control will occur before the end of this century. We've already had a preview of the disasterous results of rent control in New York City. The danger of rent control makes apartment ownership an unacceptable risk for me. The attractiveness of apartment ownership compared to houses is very minimal anyway.

Rent control in an inflationary period when expenses are allowed to rise faster than rents will create abandonment in large numbers of apartment buildings in this country. This will serve to accelerate the coming chronic shortage of affordable housing in America.

Larger apartment buildings, in my opinion, face some risky problems for the novice investor. The possibility of rent control looms as a dark cloud in our future if inflation and demand begin to drive up rents. However, with a well-organized management program, along with tenant incentives, a responsive maintenance crew, and a continuous communication channel between management and tenants, the effect of rent control can be minimized. However, well-located single family houses are probably the safest and surest way I know to build a real estate empire in the next five years.

2. *I think that duplexes, triplexes, and fourplexes—two-, three-, and four-unit buildings—offer some real advantages for those who simply can't afford high payments or any type of negative cash flow.* If you're an investor, these properties can be purchased without a monthly eat if you properly apply the techniques used in this book. In fact, you can get cash flow if the financing is structured properly and you live in one of the units.

You'll also find that these types of units are generally more liquid. Many people are interested in buying a duplex and living in one side; the money merchants generally have funds available for these units, and FHA and VA provide guarantees for one to four units. These types of guarantees keep duplexes, triplexes, and fourplexes relatively easy properties on which to place a loan. The ability to raise cash on a property will become all the more critical in the tight-money eighties.

3. Cooperative housing, such as condominiums, halfplexes, townhouses, and cooperative apartments. This type of housing generally involves an apartment-living lifestyle. It is also known as high-density housing.

Unlike the situation in the apartment lifestyle, you gain ownership rights on the individual unit you occupy. You also share common ownership of the grounds, hallways, pool, etc.

With the high cost of land and development and the growing acceptability of a more communal living style, this type of housing will play an increasingly important role during the next five years. More and more young people will see these types of units as a beginning springboard to the American dream of single family home ownership.

For others, this type of living may replace the single family home as the American housing dream. Its lower cost and generally maintenance-free lifestyle fits in with many people's housing aspirations, both young folks and retirees.

There will be adequate funds available for financing for this type of housing because it is basic shelter. This availability of funds for financing will provide the necessary degree of liquidity to ensure that the value of these units will at least keep pace with inflation. These units have some of the same benefits as the single family home. (One item to examine very carefully when buying condominiums is the monthly association or maintenance fee. These fees can be quite stiff, and often increase from year to year. Evaluate this cost in terms of your prospective future profits.) I think that cooperative units will be investment winners of the next five years.

CHAPTER 22
Financial Freedom Is a Habit

You now have a challenging choice. Will you finish this chapter, close the book, and say to yourself, "Um, lots of good ideas . . . I'll get started next week when I'm not so

busy at work . . . I'll wait until after Aunt Tilly leaves, or
. . . maybe when the kids get older, then I'll get started."
Well, I've got news for you. Next week or next year will
never come.

You will have just made a critical decision in your life.
You will have succumbed to what I call *financial bondage.*
You're not alone! Over ninety-five percent of the people
in our country will retire at age sixty-five dependent on
inadequate government handouts just to meet minimal
living expenses.

At this writing, the great Social Security system is tee-
tering on the brink of bankruptcy. Can you afford to
depend on such a system to adequately sustain you during your old age?

Retirement shouldn't be a time of financial concern. To
me, it represents a well-deserved vacation after a lifelong
contribution to society. The strange irony is that while
most people are working, they don't have the time to
travel, to explore new lifestyles, to lead a carefree exis-
tence. When people retire, they have the time, but generally don't have the financial resources.

Will you be dependent on an already overtaxed populace when you retire? Just as you are dependent on your
nine-to-five job now?

Clearly, it is your decision. Age is not a consideration.
Being young is a state of mind, not a time in life. Don't
become a financial zombie! Take action today.

FINANCIAL BONDAGE IS A HABIT

Make a clear, conscious decision today to break the habit
of financial bondage. Begin to see yourself as financially
independent. Begin to sincerely believe that you will achieve
financial freedom.

You will become exactly like the image that you hold of
yourself. If you see yourself as a financial zombie, always
financially dependent on others, the world stands ready
and willing to fulfill that vision. If you see yourself prosperous and abundant, this you will become. Whatever
self-image the mind holds has to manifest itself in reality.

Will you be prosperous or poverty stricken? It will depend on how you see yourself. Listen to your own inner thoughts. Do these thoughts express doubt and fear, or do they reflect positiveness and abundance? Your outer circumstances are a direct reflection of your inner thoughts.

If you sincerely want to improve the outer circumstances of your life, from financial bondage to financial freedom, you must change the way in which you think about yourself. After all, fear (what will happen if all my tenants move out?), doubt (can I really do it?), negativity (you can't make money in real estate anymore), and procrastination (I'll start my real estate empire when interest rates get lower) are just binding and self-defeating thinking habits.

Financial bondage is then a series of negative thinking habits. Listen to your own inner thoughts! Are they the shackles that will prevent you from experiencing wealth and abundance in your life? Will you simply put this book down after reading it because of fear, doubt, negativity, or procrastination?

That decision will be entirely up to you. However, at your disposal is an inner reservoir of unlimited creative energy that will help you transform those negative thinking habits into positive ones. Some people call this unlimited reservoir of creative energy the subconscious, the superconscious, the infinite, or God. Whatever you call it, it can aid you in transforming the circumstances of your life from financial bondage to abundance and freedom.

THE POWER TO TRANSFORM
NEGATIVE THINKING HABITS

This unlimited inner reservoir of creative energy stands willing and able to change the circumstances in your life, if only you ask.

How do you ask for this change? Very specifically, very clearly, very sincerely; and you keep asking, many times daily, until the required change occurs.

For example, let's assume that you have a fear that your tenant will move out once you buy that first property, and you'll have to make the mortage payment out of your own pocket. Write on a sheet of paper the best and the worst things that can happen if Mr. Goode Tenant moves out. Fears tend to be less burdensome when reduced to writing.

After clearly writing the best and the worst that can happen if Mr. Tenant leaves, begin to plan in writing all the existing alternatives available to you if the property should become vacant.

- Place ad in paper to rerent

- Let rental agency know of the vacancy

- Have papercarriers hand out a creatively designed flyer

- Work with mortgage holder on a delayed payment

- Lower rent; provide rent incentives

In my experience, fear diminishes as clear knowledge of a situation expands. If you clearly write out possible solutions to a possible vacancy, I think that you'll see your fear being relieved to the point where you will be able to take action and buy.

You've used your own inner creative reservoir to dispel that negative thinking habit of fear. The fear in your mind is like a jail cell; it prevents you from taking action. The key to that jail cell is your own innate creative ability to solve problems.

Once you have bought the property, you might try tapping that unlimited reservoir of creativity as insurance, so that the subdued fear concerning a vacancy doesn't rise again. Try writing on a sheet of paper something similar to the following affirmation statement: "I give Mr. Goode Tenant a good place to live, and in exchange, Mr. Goode Tenant will be a prompt-paying tenant in my house at 111 Main Street, Quincy, California, for at least the next three years."

Read this statement at least twice daily—morning and evening is best. This type of affirmation statement will help specifically focus your deepest inner thoughts toward keeping Mr. Goode Tenant in the property. By reading this type of affirmation each day, you begin to change the direction of your thoughts. As your thoughts are altered positively, so your outer circumstances will improve. Affirm what changes you desire in your life and keep affirming them, and the changes will occur.

ABUNDANCE, GOALS, AND AFFIRMATIONS

Take control of your life today! Begin to design affirmations and goals that will start you on the path to financial freedom.

Your goals don't have to be extraordinarily ambitious. You might elect to only buy one house each year for the next five years. Real estate is such an extraordinary investment vehicle that five to ten well-selected houses will spell financial freedom for those wise enough to buy now and wait for their money crop to grow.

Breaking the shackles of financial bondage is within your grasp today. Begin seeing abundance and prosperity flowing in your life; be a positive force in the world today; understand that you are responsible for the circumstances in which you find yourself; you possess an inner reservoir of creative energy that can transform any problem into a golden opportunity that will yield you unlimited riches.

You have the knowledge necessary to create your own real estate empire, starting from scratch. What will it be? Financial bondage or financial freedom?

Remember that your ideas are limitless. Individual creativity is your most valuable wealth-building tool. You'll run out of cash well before you ever exhaust the ideas available to buy property.

Take the ideas contained in this book and begin to dynamically build your real estate empire today; substitute your ideas for cash. Good luck!

Other Services, Books, and Tapes
By Ed Beckley

Services

The Million Dollar Advisory Service and The Beckley Report.
Two services that can mean the difference between success and failure for you in your real estate investing.

The Million Dollar Advisory Service.
Help for your real estate questions is just a phone call away! You get a private access code to your personal real estate wealth-building counselor. A trained advisor will answer specific questions about your real estate dealings. Expert advice like this usually costs from $100 to $125 an hour. Now you can have a year of this service as part of your subscription to the *Advisory Service* and *The Beckley Report.*

The Beckley Report.
Your private news service for behind-the-scenes tips that can add to your wealth. There's no publication in the world quite like it. Month after month it gives you the facts that will help you create wealth. It keeps you ahead of the pack by bringing you the newest, most dynamic techniques for buying and managing real estate. And it fills you in on the latest Beckley seminars, conventions, tapes, and books.

The Million Dollar Advisory Service and *The Beckley Report* are your way of accessing all the information of the Beckley System for Creating Wealth. These services will keep you in touch as the Beckley System expands into all fields of investing and entrepreneurship.

You receive both services for one annual subscription fee.
Order no. 4002-01 $77.00/year

The Beckley Catalog of Money-Making Ideas.
This catalog is a collection of the best books and tapes available on the subject of wealth-building. It includes materials by Ed Beckley and other authors who have demonstrated their ablity to turn creative ideas into wealth. A source of inspiring and wealth-producing ideas that you can put to work in your life.
Order no: 5401-01 $1.00 (This shipping and handling fee will be credited towards your first purchase from the catalog.)

TO ORDER BY PHONE
CALL TOLL FREE:
1-800-222-1090

Books

125 Irresistible Purchase Offers

One purchase offer to match each of Ed's no down payment formulas for a total of 125 different offers. Each offer is clearly written in contract form. This book can help you avoid big mistakes and save you hundreds of dollars in legal fees. Just adapt the offers to your situation and have them quickly reviewed by your lawyer.
Order no. 3103-01 $49.00

Government Gold Mines

At last! The inside information on low-interest government loans that could save you thousands of dollars in interest payment. See which programs you qualify for and get loans at as low as 3% interest. A wide variety of programs, some for the poor, some for the rich, and some for those in between. 368 pages of programs that could be gold mines for you.
Order no. 1201 $75.00

Equity Participation Agreements

Ed considers equity sharing to be one of the most powerful home-buying techniques of the '80s, but you need to make sure you have a really good equity participation agreement with your co-owner. It cost Ed over $8000 in attorney's fees to develop these agreements. Now they can serve as a building block for your equity-sharing agreements, for only a fraction of Ed's expense.
Order no. 3101-01 *$49.00*

Real Estate Forms and How to Master Them

This invaluable guide includes detailed, item-by-item descriptions of 36 different forms you're likely to need in building your real estate empire: deeds, trust agreements, contracts, reconveyances, liens, notices, and more. Bonus: glossary of over 500 important real estate terms.
Order no. 3104-01 $29.95

Iron Clad Rental Agreements

Learn from the expert. Ed developed this 8-page agreement through the years as he dealt with difficult renters. He has perfected it to the point where it can eliminate 90% of your management problems. Softcover.
Order no. 3002-01 $25.00

TO ORDER BY MAIL
SEND YOUR ORDER TO
MIDWEST FINANCIAL PUBLICATIONS
P.O. BOX 992, FAIRFIELD, IOWA 52556

Audiocassette Albums

No Down Payment Home Study Course (15 tapes, 188 page manual, plus two books: *125 Irresistible Purchase Offers* and *Equity Participation Agreements*).
This is the original full-length course on which Ed Beckley's *No Down Payment Formulas* book is based. Ed has recorded this entire 2-day seminar on audiocassette and added an extensive manual that includes valuable tools to get you started on the fast track to real estate wealth. Gives the knack, the knowledge, the feel of Ed's technique. Shows you how to quickly build a real estate empire that generates $100,000 or more each year—tax free. (Available to graduates of No Down Payment Seminars at $59.)
Order no. 1001-02 $295.00

Creating Cash Now (8 tapes, 120 page manual).
Except for his No Down Payment Home Study Course, Ed Beckley considers this tape set to be the best material he has ever recorded. Step by step, in-depth scenarios teach you how to carry out some of Ed's most creative No Down Payment strategies. This knowledge-packed series includes:
• How to pay nothing down, yet give the seller all cash.
• How to get paid $5,000-$100,000 each time you buy
• How to earn more from real estate than from your current job
• How to get paid for living in your own home
• How to put $500,000 in the bank within 5 years
(Available to graduates of No Down Payment Seminars at $99.)
Order no. 1104-01 $179.00

Five of the Best No Down Payment Techniques (8 tapes).
This album gives you a deeper understanding of the No Down Payment principles and how to make them work: "Fannie Mae" loans, lease-options, Ed's "wedge and cap" formula, equity sharing, and buying property at a discount. Also teaches you 15 different ways to take care of balloon payments.
Order no. 1103-01 $49.00

A Day with a Millionaire (9 tapes).
In this album, recorded at an all day seminar for No Down Payment graduates, Ed Beckley shares the step-by-step process of how to write nothing down purchase offers. Includes how to make $500,000 in the next three years dealing in foreclosures, how to structure lease-options, and how to exploit exotic, low-interest government loans.
Order no. 1101-01 $49.00

TO ORDER BY PHONE
CALL TOLL FREE
1-800-222-1090

The Cash In On Credit Home Study Course (24 tapes, over 800 pages of manuals and study guides).

Knowledge is power, but credit knowledge is money-making power. This course shows you how you can use credit to open the door to equity partnerships, options, auctions, repossessions, and other wealth-building opportunities. See how to get out of credit difficulties, repair credit damage, and build your credit line. Plus, you'll find out how you can create a fortune with two of today's hottest wealth-building opportunities: foreclosures and credit consulting.

Order no. 7003-03 $299.00

Money-Making Guide to Stock Market Success (This special package includes a stock market newsletter subscription, 6 tapes, and the *Investor's Buy/Sell Guide to Blue-Chip Stocks.*)

Have you always wanted to make a fortune in the stock market but didn't know how to get started? Well, here's a simple but powerful investment system that almost everyone can understand. It's based on the rise and fall of stock prices. And it doesn't matter if the prices are rising or falling. You can use this system even if you now know nothing about stocks. Over the last ten quarters this system has provided an average rate of return of 20% per year. At that rate your money doubles every 3.6 years. This is a time-tested, consistent way to build your wealth. Plus, with this system you don't need to put in a lot of time managing your investments. Let this course help take the anxiety out of investing and put you in control of your financial future.

Order no. 3302-02 $49.00

The Creation of Wealth Course (one week, in-residence seminar).

This seminar gives you the opportunity to spend one intensive week with Ed Beckley learning the secrets of wealth building. This course is only for those with an intense desire to succeed.

$1195 (Food, lodging, and course materials included.)

Melvin Powers's Mail-Order Millionaire (11 tapes, 199-page manual, plus a short course on writing winning advertisements).

You can get rich in mail order. Many people have started with almost no money and have built their mail-order business into a financial gold mine. Melvin Powers, the master teacher of mail order, shows you everything you need to get started today. Learn about Melvin Powers's million-dollar marketing strategy, how to find products that will make you a fortune, how to write money-making ads, plus much more. This is your complete guide to mail-order fortunes.

Order no. 3501-02 $149.00

TO ORDER BY MAIL
SEND YOUR ORDER TO
MIDWEST FINANCIAL PUBLICATIONS
P.O. BOX 992, FAIRFIELD, IOWA 52556

ABOUT THE AUTHOR

After graduating from San Francisco State University in 1970 with a Bachelor of Arts degree in Economics, Ed Beckley went on to get a business degree and a secondary teaching credential in 1972. He taught business courses at high school and junior college level from 1972 through 1978.

In 1975, starting from scratch and in his spare time, he bought his first real estate investment while still living in a rental. In the next three years, he proceeded to buy over two million dollars worth of real estate. In 1978, just three years after beginning his real estate program, he was able to leave his schoolteaching job and declare his financial freedom.

Today, Ed Beckley is owner and president of The Beckley Group, Inc., which produces the highly acclaimed No Down Payment Seminars, one of the most successful real estate seminars in the United States today, as well as a popular series of home study courses and the lively and informative *Beckley Report* newsletter. He has been featured in a national television special, "How To Make It In America," and also in the very powerful and moving documentary "The Millionaire Maker."

Ed has authored two other books in addition to *No Down Payment Formulas;* they are *Government Gold Mines: How to Get Low Interest Government Loans* and *Real Estate Forms and How to Master Them.* His cassette series includes "A Day with a Millionaire," "No Down Payment," and "Five of the Best No Down Payment Techniques."

Even with his demanding workload, he finds time to travel throughout the United States and Canada sharing his wealth-building and inspirational techniques, and has lectured to more than 150,000 people, in addition to the millions who viewed his TV special. Ed Beckley seems tireless in his efforts to deliver the message that keeps his programs in such high demand: The regular working man or woman can *still* make a fortune in real estate today!

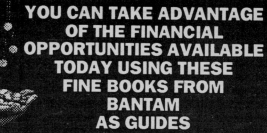